# What You Can Do With Color And Design

Simple wooden plates and boxes become priceless possessions or can be given as gifts once you decorate them.

Useful objects can be attractive too, with tasteful colors and patterns.

# Door Designs

Adapted from Pennsylvania Dutch folk art, these designs on a door give it the warmth of a personal welcome. Nor are you limited to decorating just the front door—with paint and pictures you can make your closet, kitchen, nursery, and other doors all part of your home decorating scheme.

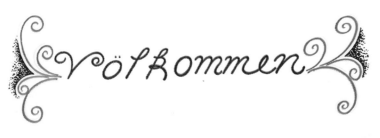

*How to Use*
# COLOR
and
# DECORATING DESIGNS
*in the Home*

# *How to Use*
# COLOR
## and
# DECORATING DESIGNS
## *in the Home*

**by**

**HOWARD KETCHAM**

GREYSTONE PRESS    NEW YORK, N. Y.

## ACKNOWLEDGMENTS

A special debt of gratitude is due *American Home* Magazine for permission to use its color illustrations in this book. The following is a list of the places where these pictures appear, with the number of each pattern (available in large size with painting instructions from the magazine): Jacket, left column: pot, No. 1006; wastebasket, No. 983; place mat, No. 949. Jacket, right column: dish, No. A938; breadboard, No. A948; box, No. A930; bottle, No. 1055; coal scuttle, No. A952. Opening color page, right side: dishes, No. A938; box at left, No. A951; boxes at right, No. 1044; sewing box, No. 1053; knife rack, No. A950; bucket, No. A952. Opening color page, left side: door designs, No. 1105; others, No. 1104. Facing page 28: kitchen, Nos. 1106 and 1107. Facing page 29: windowshade, No. 923; bunks and fireplace, No. 1012. Facing page 93: windowshade at left, No. 919; at right, No. 922; kitchen designs, No. 1018. Facing page 124: mirror and bureau, No. 970; bookcase, No. 969; butter paddles, No. 1042; modernistic salad bowl, No. A930; tin pan, No. 1035; flowered salad bowls, No. 1036. Facing page 125: antique chest, No. 980 (no patterns available for decoupage at top). Facing page 156: watering can, No. 1054; dipper, pitcher, and trays, No. A931; lunch boxes, No. 1071; coal hod, No. A952; wastepaper basket, No. 983. Facing page 157: roasting pan and bread tin, No. A951; irons, No. 1039; scoop, box, and trays, No. A947. Facing page 188: pottery pieces and salad bowl, No. 1006; napkin clips and cake plate No. 1007. Facing page 189: candle holders, No. 1048; bowl, No. 1051; pie tins, No. A939; dishes, No. A940; bottles, No. 1055; ash trays, No. A937. Facing page 220: glass, place mats, and napkins, No. 1009; luncheon cloth and napkins; No. 988; place mats, No. 1005. Facing page 221: cork mat and luncheon cloth, No. 1043; glass and place mats, No. 1008; bibs and place mat, No. A945.

The color plate of the table (facing page 92) is shown here with the permission of *Mademoiselle's Living*, and the hex signs facing pages 60 and 61 are reproduced through the courtesy of R. W. Cummings, Inc., of Lancaster, Pa., from their pamphlet *Hex Signs*.

The author wants to thank the following individuals, authors, artists, publishers, museums and organizations for permission to print authoritative data and valuable illustrative material, and for other help they have given him:

American Crayon Company; *American Fabrics Magazine*, Reporter Publications, Inc.; American Museum of Natural History; Laura Hazard Brown; Robert Bushnell; Chicago Natural History Museum; *Christian Science Monitor*; E. I. du Pont de Nemours & Co.; Esterbrook Pen Company; Donelda Fazakas; Victor Civkin, Home Bureau, General Electric Company; Max Gottschalk; Solveig Hallen; Helen Hume; C. Howard Hunt Pen Co.; W. Graham Law; *Look Magazine*; Matthew Luckiesh, *Visual Illusions and Their Application*, D. Van Nostrand; Miss Amelia Maxey; Metropolitan Museum of Art; The Meyercord Company; Kenneth M. Chapman, Assistant Director, Laboratory of Anthropology, School of American Research, Museum of New Mexico; National Gallery; National Lead Co.; Philadelphia Museum of Art; Pitman-Dreitzer and Co., Inc.; Louis Ross; Salmanson & Co., Inc.; F. Schumacher & Co.; Jean C. Simon; Adolf Spohr; Charles J. Stoner; Miss Katherine M. Harvey, Taylor Museum of the Colorado Springs Fine Arts Center; C. H. Vanderlaan; Franz Sales Meyer, *Handbook of Ornament*, Wilcox and Follett Co.

The writer wants to acknowledge his indebtedness to his long-time associates in Howard Ketcham, Inc.: Greta Hale for suggestions relating to color plans; Leon Theil for research and help in coordinating basic material; Gloria Cotz Brown and Cecelia Budd for their typing the manuscript in final form.

# ABOUT THIS BOOK

This is an age of the rebirth of individual imagination, of a spreading reaction against conventional patterns and against high costs in our living. In decorating the home, more and more housewives are becoming genuine "homemakers." Brush and paints are partly replacing the easy-to-apply decals, as people strive more and more to give creative expression to their personalities. Makeshift homes —the only available quarters for many young couples—have provided more freedom than usual for experiment. "Draw your own—be original—be yourself," is the sentiment.

This guide to the use of color and design in home decoration is planned to help the family which is stirred by this desire to create—and to show them how to save money at the same time.

It gives you simple, attractive designs and patterns and tells you how to reproduce them with such aids as a compass, ruler, and French curve, or by tracing. These decorations you can use on furniture, pottery, tinware, glassware, fabrics, tiles, floors, walls, and other surfaces.

Our approach is based largely on traditional American forms, Pennsylvania Dutch, for example. But we have not neglected others that will appeal to you— Swedish, Indian, Mexican and other attractive forms of folk and modern art from many corners of the earth.

We have combed through many private and public collections for design ideas so that this book might give you a balanced showing of what you can do in modern home decoration.

We have made all explanations as simple and direct as possible to meet the needs of an everyday family eager to take a hand in the decoration of the home. Our constant aim has been to show in fullest detail how to accomplish the results you seek, easily and economically. You don't need any great talent or detailed training to carry out the design treatments presented. The simplest early-school instruction in drawing will be background enough.

Today you needn't be afraid or ashamed to do your own. A Grandma Moses at seventy-seven takes up brush and palette, and produces primitives which excite the art world. Husband and wife in any home have the means—with their own energy and taste—to win the acclaim of friends and acquaintances. Storage warehouses proffer a rich load of unclaimed furniture which you may remake or redecorate to suit your taste and needs as a homemaker, and so do second-hand shops and unpainted wares departments.

It will be our object to show many short-cuts in the furnishing of a home, using materials readily available to an average family. We will avoid the practices of some leaders of the modern "do-and-make-do" trend which might be summarized: "If it has a mirror, remove it; if it has no mirror, add one!"

You will not find us adding color for the sake of wielding a paint brush. Often a piece is more effectively treated by bringing out the natural color of wood in the true beauty of the texture. Or an eyesore may be translated into a delight by cleaning the paint off a metal part and polishing it to bring out an attractive natural luster. But, by and large, we do hold that color can work wonders for renewing the life of an old piece, or creating life in odds and ends of materials. Remember, you see the shapes of objects only through the contrasts of color and texture—if man's vision reduced all objects to a uniform neutral gray, you would see only objects and distances.

The Pennsylvania Dutch—a mixture of German and Swiss immigrants who came over in the years before the Revolutionary War—represent the most fruitful outpouring of artistic peasant-style decoration of homes and home appliances, and it is largely to their work that we shall turn our attention for examples. These people brought with them to this country a variety of household equipment, European home style tastes, and craft skills.

Their handicraft was based on considerations of usefulness—what the modern designer would call functionalism. Color was naïve and brilliant—it was applied with freedom and sweep. They based design on the natural life about them, and the deeply felt religious life which impelled many of them to make the arduous transition from Old World to New. Thus they applied design with sincerity and intense feeling, which showed up in the finished object.

This bold and direct approach provides one of the principal appeals of the work of the Pennsylvania Dutch. While the craftsmen—the pottery makers, the weavers, the makers of iron implements and household utensils—were intent on the function, their background forced them to try to provide beautiful form and decoration. From a minimum of motifs and simple patterns they produced a variety of arrangements for admiration and satisfaction. But above all, they unconsciously followed a rule that marked the art of ancient Greece: that which is most useful is most beautiful.

As a result we find some of the best examples of their work in cooking pots, pie plates, barbers' basins, tobacco pipes, ink stands, spittoons, roofing tiles, tea canisters, cream pitchers. Most of these articles still answer the purpose for which they were intended—often better than utensils now on the market.

These highly colored, amusingly detailed utensils contributed artistic relief to the drab, monotonous, often crude appearance of early American dwellings. We can imagine from illustrations like those on the following pages how much these decorations contributed to the appearance and appeal of both furniture and utensils. Original Pennsylvania Dutch articles appear to carry with them to this day a semblance of the appeal and character of the early designers.

Because the Pennsylvania Dutch were not trained artists—as we know the word—their ideas and innovations provide a good means of introducing color styling techniques to the present-day home decorator. If these early Pennsylvania Dutch people could do so well without any art instruction or formal apprenticeship, the reader of today should be able to do even better with this simple craft. After all, we have a much greater abundance of inspiration around us today, and can turn for guidance to so many exhibits of the work of those who came before! Moreover, with modern materials, methods, and supplies, we are much more likely to achieve good results than were the people who worked from 1750 to 1850, when Pennsylvania Dutch art was at its best, and when the craftsman lacked tools, materials and guidance.

In this volume, you will find these motifs, and many others in simplified, stylized form. These breakdowns of each motif into simple line structure will serve to make the designs easy for you to apply. Color mixture is explained step by step, so that this part of your work will be easy.

Now—*go to it!* Remember, you need not be concerned with producing accurate and careful copies of the examples offered. Your handiwork is you—let your taste be your only critic!

HOWARD KETCHAM

vi

# CONTENTS

CHAPTER                                                                    PAGE

**ABOUT THIS BOOK** ........................................................................................ V

**1. COLOR DOES IT** ...................................................... 9

How to Describe Color—Hue—Value—Intensity—What Color Is—Colors in Combination—Four Rules for Grouping Colors—"Color-structor" for Selecting Harmonious Colors—Five Rules of Color Contrast—What Colors Do to Each Other—Outlining Design Figures with Color—a Color Chart for Home Decoration—Mixing Colors—the Effects of Color—Balancing Colors—Color Barometer—Chart of Color Combinations.

**2. IT'S EASY TO CREATE YOUR OWN DESIGNS** ....................... 21

Basic Lines and Shapes—Borders—the Circle—Making Decorations with Circles—the Square in Design—Starting with Design Motifs: Flowers—Drawing a Tulip—Lily—Rose—Daisy—Violet—Anemone—Thistle — Fuchsia — Forget-Me-Not — Clover — A Design of Several Flowers—How to Draw Birds—Eagle—Dove—Peacock—Pigeon—Fruit to Your Taste—Leaf Designs—Pear, Grape Cluster, and Apple—Border Decorations with Fruit—Drawing an Elephant—Gazelle—Toucan Bird—Kid—Rabbit—People with Life—the Human Body—Angels Are Easy to Draw—Pennsylvania Dutch Figures—Changing Size of Designs—Tracing Designs—How to Use a Perforating Wheel—Other Ways to Trace—Cutting Stencils—Striping a Border—A Short-Cut—Decorative Tape.

**3. FOLK DESIGNS FROM AROUND THE WORLD** ....................... 63

Themes of Folk Art—Folk Art Colors—Designs for You—Who Are the Pennsylvania Dutch?—Pennsylvania Dutch Designs—Hex Signs—Peacock, Distilfink, Rooster, Stag, etc.—Pennsylvania Dutch Colors—Swedish Design and Color—Simple Swedish Borders with Suggested Colors—Indian Designs: Borders, Birds, People, and Animals—New England Sea Chests—Mexican Motifs—Drawing a Mexican Figure—Mexican Man and Woman—Sombrero Design.

vii

**4. LETTERING FOR YOUR DESIGNS**.......................................................... 91

Where to Use Lettering—Hints on Lettering—Guide Lines—Sketch
Your Letters First—Standard Modern Gothic Alphabet and How to
Letter It—Variations of Standard Gothic—Roman Letters—Numerals
Are Decorative—Script Lettering—a Simplified Alphabet and How
to Make It—Stencil Lettering—Lettering in Hand-Writing—Messages
and Proverbs in Designs—Create Your Own Monograms—All-over
Monogram Pattern—Brushes and Paints—How to Hold the Brush—
Lettering Pens, Paints and Inks—How to Use Pens—a Prefabricated
Alphabet.

**5. DECORATING FURNITURE IN YOUR STYLE**................................. 115

Decoration Should Emphasize Construction—a Paneled Piece—Cork
Decorations—Your Hobbies in Decoration—Consider the Area—
Keep It Simple—Varying the Design—Children's Furniture—Bring
It Down from the Attic—New Use for Old Radio—Make a Secretary
— Easy Alterations — Use Imagination — Creating New Furniture
Without Hammer or Nails—a Novel Living Room Table—an Easy
Desk to Make—a Flower Cart for Your Lawn—Picture Frame Be-
comes Headboard—a Decorated Bulletin Board—Nail Kegs into Fur-
niture—How to Decorate with Paint—Sandpapering the Furniture—
Furniture with Old Finishes—Quick Way to Remove Old Finish—
Applying the Primer—the Second Coat—How to Trace the Design—
Applying Your Colors—Finishing Your Piece—Antiquing—Decou-
page—Metallic Stencils on Wood.

**6. ADVENTURES IN DECORATING TINWARE**..................................... 145

Things You Can Decorate—How to Select the Object—Materials
Needed—Practicing Your Design—Preparing the Tin—Sanding and
Priming—How to Transfer Your Design—Painting on Tin—How to
Paint Borders—How to Use Stencil Technique—Applying the Stencil
—How to Apply Overtones—How to Finish Tinware—Hints and
Warnings on Technique.

7. PAINTING TILES AND POTTERY..............................................165

Tile in Our Homes—Using Decorated Tiles on a Window Sill, Vanity Table, Bookcase, Child's Table, Tea Wagon, etc.—Applying Tile Surfaces—How to Surface a Table with Tiles—Getting Your Tile—Decorating Tiles and Pottery with Oil Paints—How to Transfer Designs—How to Paint on Burnt Clay—Permanent Ceramics Decoration—Working with Solid Paints—How to Get Metallic Effects—Firing in Your Kitchen Oven—Ceramic Powders on Glazed Wares—on Unglazed Wares—How to Apply Underglaze Colors—Applying the Design—Photographs on Tile—Collecting Autographs on Tile.

8. IT'S FUN TO PAINT ON GLASS..............................................193

How to Use Water Colors and Oil Paints to Decorate Glassware—Objects to Paint: Drinking Glasses, Dishes, Jars, Vases, Salt and Pepper Shakers, Bottles, etc.—New Ways to Paint Glass—Transparent Colors and Etched Effects—Liquid Glaze on Glass—Firing in Your Own Kitchen Oven—Reverse Painting on Glass—Materials Needed—Tracing and Painting—Advanced Painting on Glass.

9. COLORING FABRICS TO YOUR FANCY..............................................207

Clothing, Personal, and Household Accessories You Can Decorate—Starting with Textile Colors—Hints for Combining Colors—How to Cut Stencils—Design Ideas for Clothes and Home Furnishings—Other Uses of Textile Colors — Oil Paints on Fabric — Materials Needed—Preparing the Cloth and Design—How to Paint.

10. COLOR AND DESIGN FOR YOUR ROOMS..............................................223

Selecting Colors and Designs—Dress Up Your Garage—Designs for Your Floors—Spatter-Dash Floors—Selecting the Colors—Applying Spatter Color—a Border for the Spatter-Dash Floor—Applying a Floor Design by Stencil—Geometric Patterns—Novel Borders—Wallpaper on Floors—Color for Walls—Color Combinations and Moods—Painting on Walls—How to Fill in Cracks—How to Apply Stencils—Wallpaper and New Materials—for the Children's Room—Colors

That Children Prefer—Selecting Designs—Painting Murals on Plaster—Masonite Cutouts—Repeating Designs on Walls—Doily Canopy—Picture Window for Stained Glass Effect—the Playroom—How to Decorate the Bar—Card Motifs—Use Your Hobbies as Themes—Painted Windows in the Basement Playroom—the Bathroom—Designs with Fabric—Painted Shower Curtains—the Kitchen—Recipes on Your Walls—Food and Utensils in Caricature—Bedroom, Living Room, and Breakfast Nook — the Attic — How to Use Decals — on Blinds—Designs on Doors—Stair Risers—Luminous Paints on Stairs and Lamps—a Last Word: Color in Your Life.

*How to Use*
# COLOR
and
# DECORATING DESIGNS
*in the Home*

# CHAPTER 1

# COLOR
# Does It

Few elements in our natures give us greater or more varied pleasure than the ability to see color. We have only to picture life in terms of a black-and-white motion picture film to realize the truth of this fact.

Perhaps you regard the correct use of color as a mystery. It need not be one. When you have read a few pages, you will see that it is possible to select colors for your home without fear—and that you can use them to express your own personality.

To show how important color is, we need only point out that you see the shapes of objects largely because of differences in colors. For example, notice the chair against the wall of your living room. If the chair—wood, upholstery and all—were of exactly the same color as the wall, how well do you think you would see it?

The answer is, you would hardly notice it! Only the difference in texture

between the materials in the chair and the wall surface—and possible shadows—would give it away.

## HOW TO DESCRIBE COLOR

To start learning to use color, you must first learn how to describe it.

Imagine that you have called a friend on the telephone, to describe the color of a new material you have purchased to slip-cover your living room pieces. You want to ask what color should be used for the draperies you are planning to buy. How would you describe the color of your material?

Don't be embarrassed if you find it impossible to do so. As great a writer as Robert Louis Stevenson was, he found it beyond his talents to describe the pink of the coral on his Tahiti island home, in writing to a friend in London for furniture fabrics to go with it. It is only since Stevenson's time that we have had a way of describing color.

There are three things about color that need explanation, to help in describing it: hue, value, and intensity.

### Hue

Hue is a quality which sets a color apart from other colors, such as: red, orange, yellow, green, turquoise, blue, purple, magenta. You will see that it is easy to set the different colors in neat order, on the basis of hue.

### Value

Value refers to the lightness or darkness of a color. A red may be very light —in the variation we call pink—if it is mixed with white. The same red may be very dark—in the shade we call maroon —if it is mixed with black. Every hue therefore includes a variety of values ranging from light to dark. Light values are also called high values—to impress this fact on your memory, simply imagine the lightness of 'a balloon which carries it high in the air. Dark values are low values.

### Intensity

The intensity refers to the purity—or lack of grayness—in a color. An emerald green has great intensity—it has no grayness in it. An olive, on the other hand, is grayish-green.

Some hues are most brilliant in light values—others in dark values. For example, a certain light yellow is the most brilliant (possesses the greatest inten-

sity) of the yellows. Maximum intensity of blue or green is obtained in certain dark values of these hues.

Now, look at your carpet. Can you identify its hue fairly closely? Is it a light version—or dark? Is it pure—or grayed? When you can tell someone these things about a color, you can put a pretty clear picture in his mind.

Now you can also use the color, with some understanding of what it's all about. You can apply the simple rules which are given in this chapter to help you use color successfully in your home. All you need is a good imagination, a sense of fitness, and a feeling for a pleasing appearance in the combination of colors, design motifs, and layout—for the fullest enjoyment of color depends upon your ability to see colors accurately and to combine them agreeably.

### WHAT COLOR IS

We see color as the result of the fact that all materials reflect light. What we see as a red kerchief is red only because the dye materials in the cloth reflect red from the rays of light; all other colors in the rays of light are absorbed by the cloth. The dye materials which cause the reflection of the red rays of light, and which absorb the blue, yellow, green and other rays of light, are called pigments. These pigments give the color to our paints, and even to our flesh.

Pigments are mixed in different combinations to give us different colors. For example, one pigment gives us a yellowish red that differs from another, more purplish red. The many different combinations we can use give us endless variety in working with color.

## COLORS IN COMBINATION

When two or more colors are used together, one of two things happens:

1. They will be harmonious, which is pleasant.

2. They will be discordant, which is unpleasant.

To understand how to pick complementary colors to use together, imagine that all colors are located on a circle, or "color wheel." They follow in clockwise order: red, orange, yellow, green, blue-green, blue, purple, magenta.

### Four Rules for Grouping Colors

Here are four rules for grouping colors successfully:

1. Each color and its opposite on the color wheel (for example, red and blue-green) have strong contrast. In using two opposite colors, be sure they are not too bright, or displayed together in too large areas, or you will have a clash. If one color or both are somewhat grayed, they look better together.

2. Each color and its neighbor (red and orange, blue and blue-green, etc.) arranged together, insure mellow beauty.

3. A combination of three colors (two adjacents with an opposite) is obtained by drawing a triangle over your color wheel. Where the triangle meets the color wheel, the corresponding colors (for example, red, blue and green) are harmonious. The use of three colors is always more interesting than two.

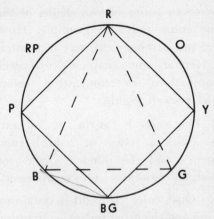

### COLORSTRUCTOR

In this Colorstructor there are eight color families (red, orange, yellow, green, blue-green or turquoise, blue, purple, and red-purple or magenta). Colors which are opposite on the Colorstructor circle, such as red and blue-green, are complementary, and create the greatest possible degree of color contrast. A jarring effect is apt to result from use of two strong complementary colors in equal areas. Generally, it is best to gray one of the two colors in such a combination, and to use the grayed color in a greater area of the surface decorated than the strong color.

Attractive combinations of three colors are obtained by drawing a triangle like the dotted-line figure in the circle above. Start with a color and its opposite—in this case the red and blue-green—and form your triangle with the points resting on red and the two colors adjacent to the blue-green, the blue and green. Or, the triangle may be formed with the blue-green, orange and red-purple; rotate the triangle if you wish other combinations of three colors. In a three-color combination, one color should be dominant.

To provide a four-color harmony, construct a square within the Colorstructor by joining the alternate color families on the rim of the color wheel; this square, too, may be rotated.

4. Color variations within a single color family look well together (for example, pink and red or maroon; orange and brown; yellow and olive).

### Five Rules of Color Contrast

You thus obtain a harmonious color scheme by using various shades of the same color—reds, for example. However, this arrangement may lack interest. Here are some simple rules to cover combinations of contrasting colors which go well together:

1. One color is "warm" or "advancing" (with a yellow or reddish component), and the other is "cold" or "receding" (contains a blue component).

2. One color is light (containing white) and the other is dark (containing black).

3. One color is grayed and the other is pure (bright, with little gray to tone down the intensity).

4. One color is used in a large area, the other in a small portion of the design.

5. One color is the complementary color to the other. We have noted what the complementary colors are on our color wheel.

### What Colors Do to Each Other

When two colors are placed side by side they will "influence" each other; they will appear different from the way each looks by itself.

For example, a light red, placed beside a dark yellow, will appear darker and bluer; the yellow will look greenish. You must be as careful in selecting two colors to go together as you would be in selecting a frame to go with your favorite painting.

Luckily, as you will see, it has been possible to set up a chart of colors for you to use, which will cut down the danger of using colors which do not go well together.

But even in using the colors of this chart, some combinations can be picked out which would not harmonize. You can get around this danger, however, by using a third color, which has the effect of tying the color scheme together attractively.

## OUTLINING DESIGN FIGURES WITH COLOR

Here are seven rules which can be applied in separating the color used on a design figure from its background, to heighten the effect created:

1. Any design figure is made to stand out against the background color by outlining it in gold, silver, white or black, the choice depending on which provides the greatest contrast with the background color.

2. Colored figures on a white background need no edging if their color is not too light; colored figures on a black background may also be effective without an edging if the color is not too dark.

3. Colored figures on a background in contrasting color (red on green, for example) are more prominent if outlined in a lighter or darker version of the background color (that is, red on green should be outlined in a darker or lighter green).

4. Colored design figures on a light

background color, like gold, should be outlined in a darker variation of the design color (for example, green on gold should be outlined in dark green).

5. If both design color and background color are dark, an outline in a light color may be needed.

6. Gold stands out best with black outline, on any color background.

7. The design figure has less need of outline if the background and design colors are selected to take advantage of the laws of contrast, which were given previously.

In fact, by following the laws of contrast, or by using the colors on the chart provided, you will find it easy to dispense with an outline for figures in your decorative designs, unless you desire one.

## A COLOR CHART
## FOR HOME DECORATION

For the purposes of this book, a chart of nineteen colors is offered for your use in painting decorative designs. These are colors that will be particularly effective on the Pennsylvania Dutch, American Indian, Mexican, and Swedish designs you will find in this book.

These colors withstand the ravages of use and soilage. They are also colors that are not too bright to use in the home.

At the same time, they go well together. Your first consideration in using colors together is to be sure they are harmonious. A color is bad if it is inappropriate or if it is used in combination with other colors which do not harmonize with it.

The chart is so arranged that any four or five colors touching in any direction or directions are in harmony. For example a broken line through Colors No. 2, 6, 13 and 14 would touch on four colors which may be used successfully in a color scheme.

These colors do not comprise a complete color chart for all purposes. They do provide a chart of colors that may be used in homes decorated with simple basic conventional design motifs, which are attractive and easy to select and paint.

Nine of these nineteen colors may be purchased ready-made in tubes, and the others can be made from these (together with black and white). For example, Color No. 7 is produced by mixing Nos. 6, 8 and white; Color No. 9 is made from Nos. 1, 8 and white; Color No. 10 is made from Nos. 8, 5, or black, and white. Color No. 11 is from Nos. 1, 8 and 13. And so on. The instructions with the chart tell how to make each.

## MIXING COLORS

At some time you may desire to use a color not on the chart, in order to duplicate a color from your favorite painting, from your upholstery, or some other source. To help you with such a project, here are some simple facts about mixing colors.

All colors may be derived from a total of no more than eight basic colors: red, orange, yellow, green, blue, purple, and black and white.

# YOUR COLORS

## —AND HOW TO MAKE THEM

| COLOR NAME | IDENTIFYING NUMBER ON CHART | PIGMENTS NEEDED TO PRODUCE THE COLOR |
|---|---|---|
| Yellow | 1 | Chrome Yellow Medium |
| Orange | 2 | Chinese Vermilion |
| Purple-Blue | 3 | New Blue or Ultramarine |
| Indian Red | 4 | Carmine or Alizarin Crimson |
| Dark Brown | 5 | Vandyke Brown or Burnt Umber |
| Maroon | 6 | Burnt Sienna |
| Light Brown | 7 | Burt Sienna (6), Yellow Ochre (8), White |
| Buff | 8 | Yellow Ochre |
| Light Yellow | 9 | Chrome Yellow (1), White, Yellow Ochre (8) |
| Ivory | 10 | Yellow Ochre (8), White and touch of Black or Brown (5) |
| Olive | 11 | Green (13), Chrome Yellow (1), Yellow Ochre (8) |
| Leaf Green | 12 | Green (13), Chrome Yellow (1), White |
| Forest Green | 13 | Viridian or Chrome Green |
| Light Green | 14 | Green (13), White, touch of Chrome Yellow (1) |
| Dark Blue | 15 | Paine's Gray or Indigo |
| Light Blue | 16 | Green (13), White, Blue (3) |
| Pink | 17 | Burnt Sienna (6), White and touch of Chrome Yellow (1) |
| Silver Gray | 18 | Black and White and touch of Paine's Gray (15) or Brown (5) if needed |
| Rose | 19 | Carmine (4), Burnt Sienna (6) and White |

Nos. 1, 2, 3, 4, 5, 6, 8, 13 and 15 are colors which may be found already mixed in tubes under the names to the right of the numbers. However, these pigments are apt to vary more or less in the products of different manufacturers and even in those of the same manufacturer from time to time, so sometimes you may have to add a little black or white or brown to obtain the exact shade shown on the chart. A slight variation of tint, however, is not too important in Pennsylvania Dutch designs, which allow for considerable leeway within their own range of color.

Nos. 7, 9, 10, 11, 12, 14, 16, 17, 18 and 19 are made up of the other pigments listed above, plus black and white, as indicated. There is no simple way of showing the exact proportions needed, the best method being trial and experiment.

14

You can obtain the colors you want by following these formulas:

1. Red and yellow make orange.
2. Red and blue make purple.
3. Blue and yellow make green.
4. Four parts of orange and one part of green make citron.
5. Four parts of green and one of purple make olive.
6. Four parts of orange and olive make russet.

Vary the proportions and you change the colors accordingly. And you can make further changes in tints and shades by adding white or black. For example:

1. Yellow and white produce pale yellow.
2. Yellow and black produce bottle green.
3. Red and white produce pink.
4. Red and black produce brown.
5. Blue and white produce pale azure blue.
6. Blue and black produce indigo.
7. Purple and white produce lilac or lavender.
8. Purple and black produce maroon brown.
9. Green and white produce pale green.
10. Green and black produce dull dark green.
11. Orange and white produce flesh tints.
12. Orange and black produce olive brown.
13. Citron and white produce hay and sage green.
14. Citron and black produce dark stone gray (greenish).
15. Russet and white produce terra cotta.
16. Russet and black produce brown.
17. Olive and white produce greenish gray.
18. Olive and black produce deep green black shades.
19. White and black produce grays.

These results, again, depend on the variation of each color you put into the mixture. For example, the yellow which would combine with black to produce a bottle green must contain a certain amount of green to begin with. The same yellow mixed with blue will produce a lighter, more intense green because blue also contains some green.

## THE EFFECTS OF COLOR

Wonderful indeed are the effects of color. Mankind has built up so many mental associations in regard to colors that we cannot use them without considering the meanings they will have in other people's minds.

For this reason you can use color to gain specific effects.

Some colors are lively, some are somber. Compare the bright colors of a Mexican or an Indian blanket with the mauves and deep browns or greens of a typical Victorian living room of the 1890's.

Some colors are stimulating, some relaxing.

Some colors go well together, others are discordant. You have seen how to avoid discord in combining colors.

Some colors are said to be "warm," others "cold." All colors that contain red or yellow are "warm," while those that do not are "cold." Colors which are said to be "warm" are also described as "advancing," while the "cold" colors are "receding." An object in an "advancing" color, seen across the room, appears to be nearer than an object in a "receding" color, although the two may be identical in size and shape, and equally distant from you. Color effect may make a distance appear to vary as much as one foot in twenty.

Colors influence apparent size and weight. A light-colored object looks larger than the same object painted black, maroon or a deep brown.

Colors which are more intense appear heavier. For example, take the two colors on the scales in the accompanying illustrations. One is pure (of high intensity) and the other is grayed. An equal area of each throws the balance scale down heavily on the side of the more intense color. By reducing the area of intense color used and increasing the area devoted to the grayed color, you can achieve balance in your color relationships.

Some colors will conceal soilage, or disguise dirt and wear; others will readily show up the ravages of soot, dust, and the rubbing of two objects against each other. In selecting colors for use in your home, you should take into consideration the amount of handling the object to be decorated will receive. In most homes, frequent repainting and short-term use of furnishings are not part of the natural scheme of things, and we have kept this constantly in mind in recommending colors and designs.

So dominant are the impressions created by color that we can take many an object whose basic styling and shape are not appealing by today's standard of taste, and transform it into a suitable, attractive item of home furnishing.

Imagine a dresser topped by a mirror mounted in an ornately scrolled frame. There are two ways to use color to give the piece a modern touch. Paint the scrollwork so that the frame does not stand out against the wall background; or use a combination of gay colors to create attractive and amusing designs in the scrollwork.

All the effects of color on our moods and reactions are based on age-old associations. Primitive man knew when fruit was ripe—by its color. He associated the red of fire with heat and warmth, the blue of the sky with purity, the dark blue of night with frigidity, the green of plants with freshness and life, the golden yellow sunlight with light and gaiety. We make similar associations today. Think of all the phrases you use which describe moods in terms of color: "green with envy," "feeling blue," "seeing red," "purple with rage," "in a brown study," etc.

Just as we speak of primary colors in mixing paints, we can speak of "psychological primary colors." These are:

1. *Red, orange:* Hot—warm—stimulating—active
2. *Yellow, yellow-green:* Fresh—dry—crisp—relaxing
3. *Green, blue:* Cold—cool—chilling—passive

16

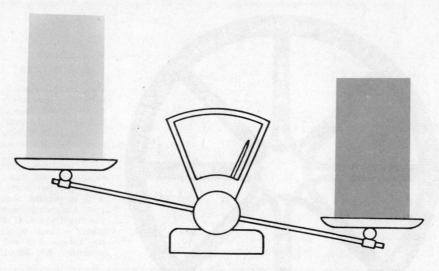

## BALANCING COLORS

*(Top)* An area of strong color overpowers a similar-sized adjacent area in subdued color. Therefore you will find it desirable to make sparing use of strong colors, employing just enough of such colors to balance or accent larger subdued areas. *(Bottom)* An area of approximately one half of the stronger color balances an area twice as large finished in the subdued color.

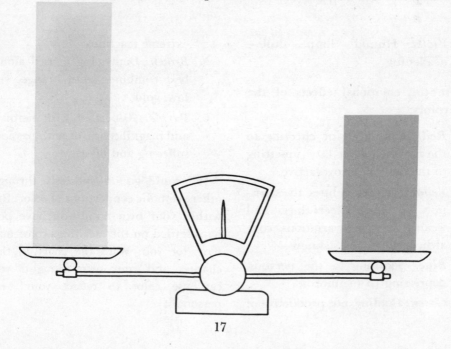

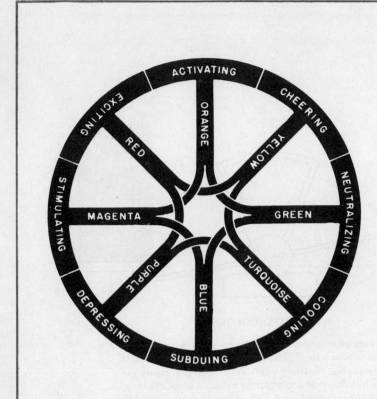

**COLOR BAROMETER**

Showing the relationship of various colors to the psychological reactions of the individual. In selecting colors for decorative design, as in selecting color treatments for furniture and basic features of your room, it is important that you first determine the mood you wish to create — then select the colors that will produce the effect.

4. *Violet:* Humid — limp — dull — deadening

Here the emotional effects of the basic colors:

1. *Red:* Stimulating or cheering to the melancholy or lazy, upsetting to the nervous or overactive
2. *Yellow:* In certain hues, the sensation of glory, cheerfulness and wealth; in other variations, cowardice, cheapness, sickness
3. *Blue:* Soothing to the nervous, depressing to the morose
4. *Green:* Cooling, not productive of extreme reactions
5. *Brown:* Depressing if used alone, best combined with orange, yellow, gold
6. *Purple:* Associated with heroism and magnificence, or with passion, suffering and mystery

We could go on endlessly through other symbolic connections of color. But within your own mind you have perhaps settled on the meanings color may have for you. With the chart in this chapter and your own thoughts you can use color to reflect your own personality.

# USING COLORS IN COMBINATION

| Some Good Combinations | Fair Color Combinations | Poor Color Combinations |
|---|---|---|
| Scarlet and turquoise | Vermilion and chartreuse | Scarlet and green |
| Scarlet and blue | | Scarlet and yellow |
| Vermilion and purple | | Scarlet and violet |
| Vermilion and blue | | |
| Light peach and dark violet | | Orange and purple |
| Orange and blue | Orange and green | |
| Red-orange and blue-green | Orange-yellow and purple | |
| Golden yellow and blue | Orange-yellow and turquoise | |
| | Yellow and green or violet | |
| | Yellow and turquoise | Yellow and bright red |
| Chartreuse and violet | | |
| Chartreuse and royal blue | | |
| Chartreuse and coral pink | Lime yellow and purple | Lime yellow and turquoise |
| Lime yellow and blue | | |
| | Green and vermilion | Green and purple |
| Turquoise and violet | Turquoise and blue | Turquoise and green or yellow-green |

COLOR AND DECORATING
DESIGNS MAKE HOUSEHOLD
OBJECTS GAY AND ATTRAC-
TIVE.

# CHAPTER 2

# It's Easy to Create
# YOUR OWN DESIGNS

Just as many colors are made by combining other colors, so designs are combinations of design elements. It is easy to combine simple lines and shapes to make effective design figures. You don't even have to be good at free-hand drawing. In this chapter we shall show you how, with the aid of a few simple drawing devices, you can create out of basic strokes and curves a wide variety of figures—flowers, animals and people. The designs you will find here are all reduced to essentials—you can fill in more details or "embroidery" as you please.

Getting your designs on the things you want to decorate may present some problems. At the end of this chapter we shall explain how to enlarge or reduce your designs, how to cut stencils, and ways of transferring your designs.

All decoration is derived from seven basic lines; either singly or in combination:

The straight line

The curved line

The wavy line

The broken line (or zigzag)

The circle

The semicircle

The letter *S*

21

Semicircles and smaller curves combine to make a rainbow-capped landscape. You can easily rearrange the elements of this design to suit your taste, or use it in its present form as a decoration on a tray or a canister.

(Below)

### QUICK DRAWING

A butterfly is quickly drawn by combining a few basic lines.

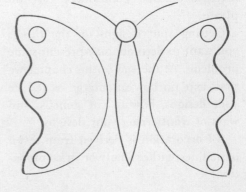

These elements may be combined in decorative treatments on a surface—flat, like a tray or desk top; curved, like a canister set or a chair leg; or squared off, like a chest or an Empire period dresser leg.

Geometric forms and the objects found in nature are basically a combination of these lines. So are all the decorative motifs adapted from human

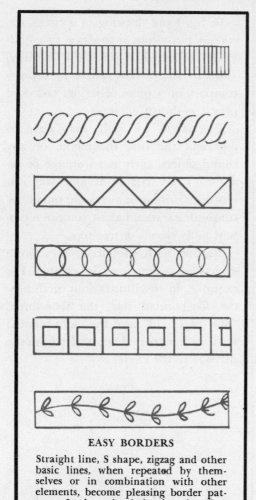

**EASY BORDERS**

Straight line, S shape, zigzag and other basic lines, when repeated by themselves or in combination with other elements, become pleasing border patterns. In these simple borders the effect is rather formal.

**BORDERS WITH LIFE**

In planning a border treatment which has life and motion, remember that it is a good rule to combine "still" elements—such as a circle or a straight line—with a continuous "moving" line like the zigzag or curve.

experience.

For example, wavy lines create a basic image of the sea. A jagged or wavy line joined to a curved line makes a leaf. Try it and see. Then do another, a short distance away, with the two curved lines roughly parallel. You now have two leaves. Between them, insert two curved lines, forming a canoe-shaped object. A circle at one end of the "canoe" . . .

**SIMPLE LINES MAKE A PICTURE**

Wavy lines suggest the sea—simple zigzag lines are birds in flight.

a pair of curved lines at either side . . . behold! the two "leaves" and the "canoe" combine into a butterfly.

23

## HOMEMADE COMPASS

A piece of string, a tack, and a pencil permit you to draw a larger circle than can be made with a compass.

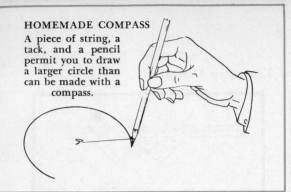

## THE CIRCLE

In free-hand drawing of a circle, the correct technique is to draw two half-circles, attached. If you are a beginner, you can obtain best results by using a compass, or a piece of string, tack and pencil as shown.

The circle, by itself, may serve to represent the sun, the moon, or any round object, such as an orange or an apple. Take half of it and you can create a rainbow or a crescent moon. By combining several halves, you can represent puffy clouds or tree tops.

Starting with the circle, an infinite variety of designs may be created. For example, in the illustrations, note how the five-pointed star, the six-pointed "Star of David" and the eight-pointed star, are constructed accurately from the division of the circle.

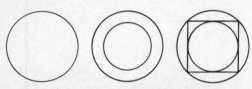

## SQUARE IN A CIRCLE

The circle is your guide for drawing a perfect square. Within one circle, draw another two-thirds the width of the first. Then draw a line touching the inner circle on each of four sides, as shown.

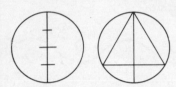

## TRIANGLE IN A CIRCLE

To draw an equal-sided triangle, run a line down the center of a circle and divide this line in quarters. Rule a line across the bottom quarter, and two more lines from the ends of that one to connect with the top.

### DESIGN OF CIRCLES

Small circles grouped around a large one make an attractive decoration.

### SLICING THE CIRCLE

Slice a circle with parallel lines and the result is this handsome design.

## SIX-POINTED STAR MAKES DESIGN

Follow the outlines of the six-pointed star to develop this varied and interesting "hex" sign, suitable for decorating many objects.

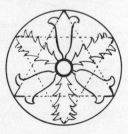

## COMBINING CIRCLES

You can combine circles in many different ways to create your own designs.

## THE CIRCLE IS YOUR FRAME

Starting with the circle, you can create perfectly proportioned shapes and stars of different types for use in decoration. Be sure to measure each part carefully.

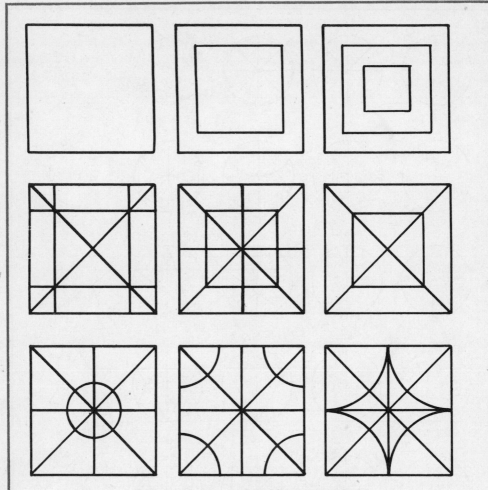

**FOR OVER-ALL PATTERNS OR BORDERS**

Starting with a simple square, it is easy to create a variety of designs merely by dividing it. One approach is to use the square-within-square technique. Circle-within-square or arc-within-square designs are indicated in the bottom row. These developments on the square design are suited for over-all patterns, and may be used as well for border treatment.

### The Square in Design

The regular four-sided figure, or square, provides an easy means of picturing a box, the framework of a house, or other figures.

Suppose we try dividing a square into compartments in various ways. The principal lines we use to create designs and subdivisions of the square are the diagonals, which connect opposite corners, and transverse lines connecting the centers of each of the four sides.

In the illustration, note how these connecting lines are used to form in-

26

creasingly complex figures. The famous "hex" signs of the Pennsylvania Dutch, which were used to ornament barns and building walls, are based on such subdivisions of squares and circles. As you will see, they form a rich source of design inspiration.

Observation of these divisions of squares and of circles will not only help to create design motifs, but will serve as a guide to your arrangement of design figures on the surface of table

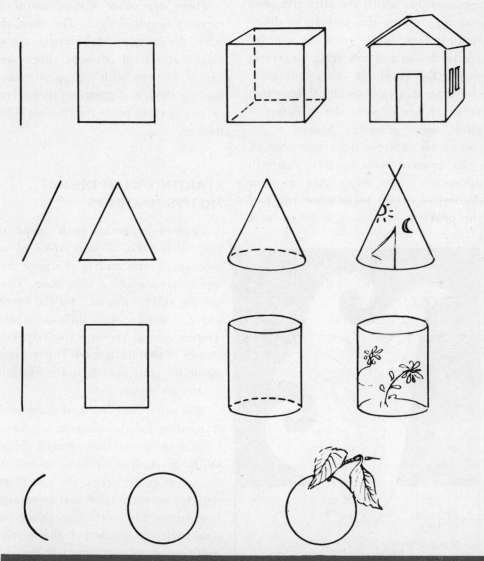

**LINES INTO DESIGNS**

Cube, triangle, cone, cylinder and other shapes are all built by combining straight lines and curves. And it takes only a few strokes to convert these shapes into pictorial objects for your designs.

27

tops, doors, cabinet drawers, etc.

For example, to determine a good size for a border design on a table top, notice the relationship of interior and exterior squares in the illustration; these provide a variety of proportional relationships which are attractive, and you may follow this picture in determining how much space to use for border design and how much for central panel. For emphasis and eye interest, the central area should be decorated with a figure of some size—a square, a circle, other geometric figures, or designs from nature or from other sources.

Experiment with squares. You will appreciate their importance in your decorative design plans when you face the problem of putting a design on a square table top, for example. You may plan to tile a table top with ceramic tile squares you have decorated yourself. Put four of the squares into a squared pattern of the type shown, and you have a "design within a design."

There are other shapes useful in creating simple designs. The cone, the cube, the cylinder, the triangle, are all combinations of straight lines and curves. You can, with appropriate coloring, use them as decorations themselves, or as a starting point for creating other designs.

## STARTING WITH DESIGN MOTIFS—FLOWERS

Three inexpensive tools make up your artist's kit, if you prefer to use mechanical aids and to postpone freehand drawing till a later date. These are the ruler, compass, and the French curve. There are many different types of French curves; the one you require is shown in the illustration. It is a curved guide for your pencil, and is available at any art supply store.

The ruler, compass, and curve make it possible for the amateur to draw a large number of basic design shapes. With this simple equipment, you can reproduce to perfection the seven basic design lines mentioned earlier—straight line, curved line, wavy line, zigzag line, semi-circle, circle, and S shape. Your mechanical aids, as you will see, also help you to achieve precisely the proportions you want in the various parts of your designs.

**FRENCH CURVE**

Many different types of French curves are available at art supply stores. The one pictured, often described as "No. 29," provides a great variety of curve edges for your use.

# Color Cheer for the Kitchen

This kitchen and its furnishings have been decorated as a unit. The larger designs form a gay and interesting panorama of Pennsylvania Dutch life as a modern person sees it, with typical patterns of flowers and birds on the smaller surfaces. Even the table and clock over the sink have been fitted into the scheme.

A baptism, with the church in the background, a romantic boy and girl, the family at dinner—all these designs show a sense of humor as bright as the colors used.

*(Right)* Bunks in a summer place are framed with a colorful floral design that could also be used to decorate windows.

*(Above)* A window-shade in a nursery is the background for simple, sparkling designs that appeal to a child.

## Color Makes a House a Home

*(Right)* The same design appearing around the bunks above serves here as a border for a fireplace.

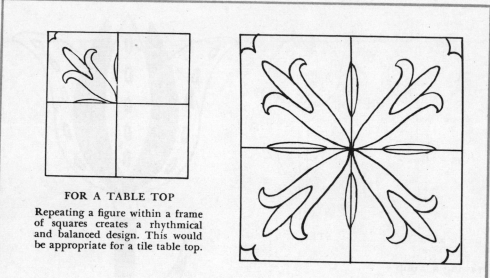

### FOR A TABLE TOP

Repeating a figure within a frame of squares creates a rhythmical and balanced design. This would be appropriate for a tile table top.

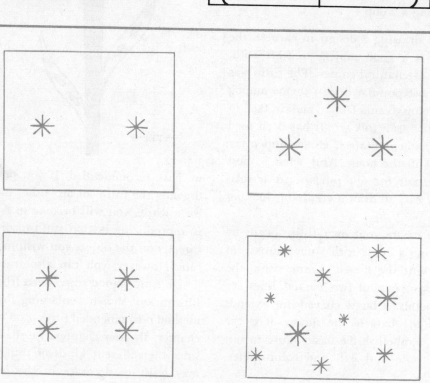

### STARS IN DESIGNS

Which of these designs is more attractive—and why? Because balance is likely to prove monotonous, designs on the left have less appeal. The variety in the shape and placement of the stars in the bottom right design makes for more eye interest than in the one above it, although the three stars are pleasingly arranged.

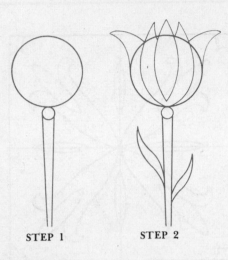

STEP 1          STEP 2

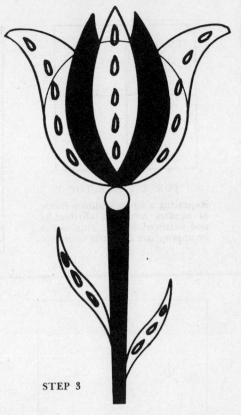

STEP 3

## Drawing a Tulip

For drawing a design in earnest, the tulip is a good subject to start with, using mechanical guides. The tulip was the most popular design theme among the Pennsylvania Dutch, and, in fact, in all European folk art. It has been used to ornament pottery, chests, and other pieces in the home. And, what is most important for our purpose, it is relatively easy to draw a creditable-looking tulip.

To create your own tulip, begin by drawing a circle with your compass, to represent the flower. Again, using the compass, extend two curved lines for the petals. A larger curved line extends from the base of the flower—it is the stem. Embellish the basic figure to suit your taste and skill and color preference.

Complicated? Not really! You can master it readily, now that you have broken down the figure into a few basic lines, and have the three simple tools—ruler, compass and French curve—which

we have recommended. If you practice drawing the tulip—or any other motif—for a while, you will become so skillful in reproducing it, that you can draw it directly on the object you wish to decorate. However, you can also trace the design from a good copy—even from the illustration shown, enlarging by the method recommended further on in this chapter. In later chapters we shall consider the different kinds of things you may want to decorate in the home—furniture, ceramics, metalware and others. In each chapter you will find a detailed explanation of how to trace designs onto different materials. The basic principle is the same in any case.

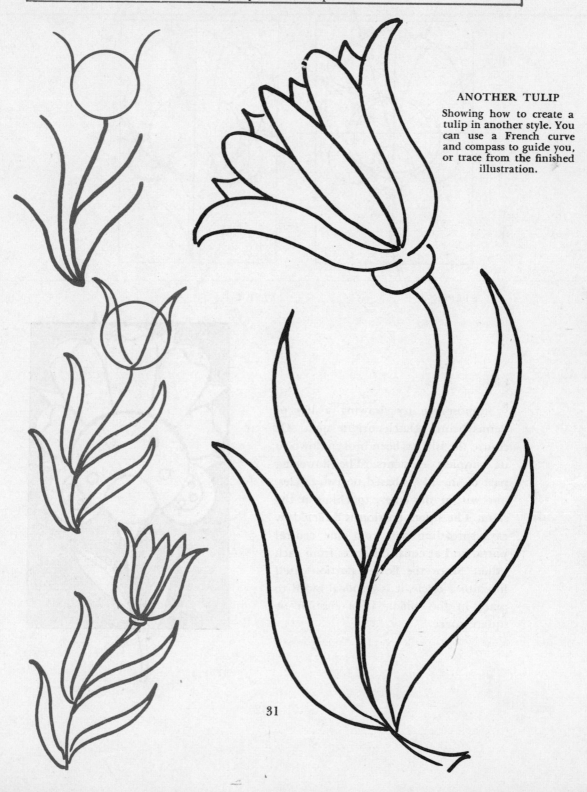

**ANOTHER TULIP**

Showing how to create a tulip in another style. You can use a French curve and compass to guide you, or trace from the finished illustration.

31

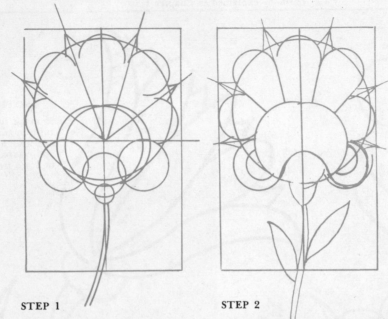

STEP 1          STEP 2

## Lily

Suppose we try drawing a lily of Pennsylvania Dutch origin next. Of course the lily has been broken down to its simplest elements. The flowering part of the lily is based on two circles, one within the other, touching at the stem. The upper portion is directed by rays spreading out from one central point, and at equal distances from each other. Since the flower portion itself fits into a circle, it is an ideal motif to place in the middle of a circular or square space.

STEP 3

## Rose

The rose illustrated is also basically an embellishment of two circles. Make these with a compass, and base them on the same center point. Curved lines to make the petals are easy to draw.

The rose, too, will look effective in the center of a square area or a rectangle—on a jewel chest, for example—or it can be used as a repetitive motif.

STEP 3

STEP 1

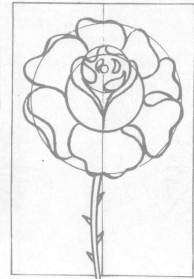

STEP 2

## Daisy

Two circles based on the same center provide the guide-lines for a daisy. The distance between the two circles determines the length of the petal, but only roughly. If they are á bit uneven, they look more natural. You can draw in the petals and the leaf neatly by using the right slots in your French curve.

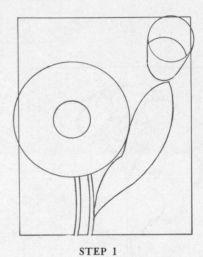

STEP 1

STEP 2

STEP 3

STEP 1

STEP 2

STEP 3

### Violet

To draw the violet shown, the basic tools you need are your French curve and compass. Use the French curve to achieve the graceful lines of the stem. The compass gives the general outline for the flower and the leaf—each is a circle. The flower itself is composed of five small circles around another circle of the same size — these become the petals. Draw parallel lines through the center of the leaf and connect these to the stem. Notice that the flower and its leaf are comprised in a circle of the same size.

35

## Anemone

You make the central part of the anemone with two small circles, one within the other. Next, surround these with a larger circle—all three circles being centered on the same point. Distribute the petals from the center to the outside circle, creating a geometric effect. The outermost circle is drawn in lightly, to serve only as a guide to provide equal length and spacing for the petals—it is not actually part of the finished design.

STEP 1

STEP 3

STEP 2

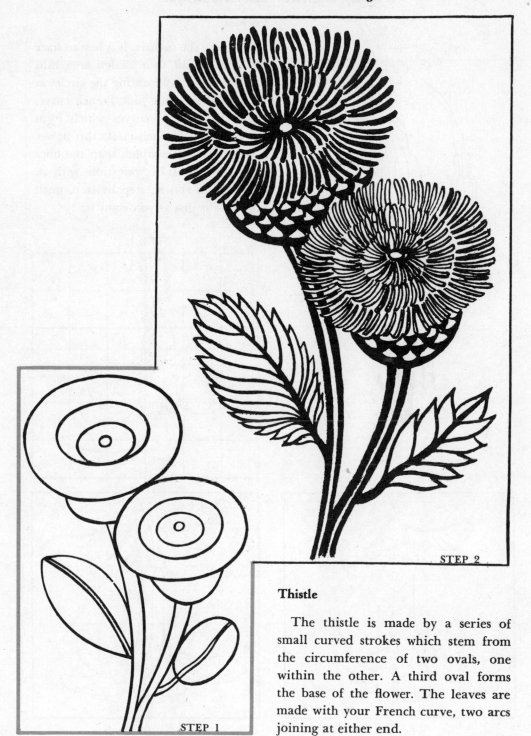

STEP 2

STEP 1

### Thistle

The thistle is made by a series of small curved strokes which stem from the circumference of two ovals, one within the other. A third oval forms the base of the flower. The leaves are made with your French curve, two arcs joining at either end.

37

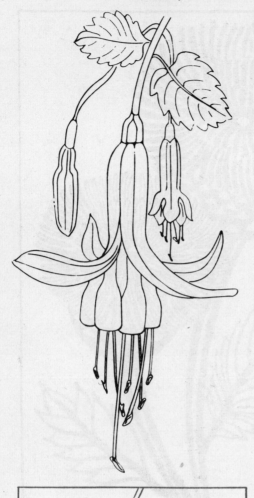

### Fuchsia

To make the fuchsia, it is best to start by blocking off your design area into small squares and locating the circles as shown. Then, with your French curve, draw the graceful curves which form the petals of the fuchsia. As this flower is a little more complex than the ones shown before, take your time with it. Build it up slowly, step by step, until you have it just as you want it.

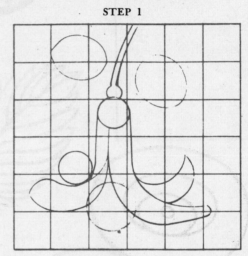

STEP 1

STEP 2

STEP 3

38

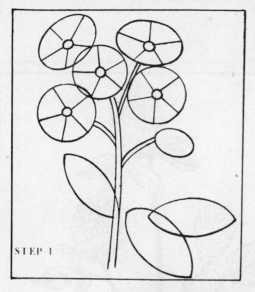

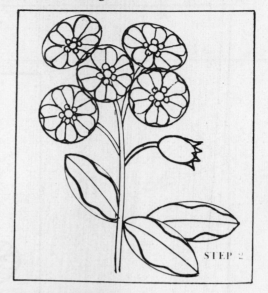

## Forget-Me-Not

The forget-me-not is a grouping of five small flowers assembled together in any pleasing arrangement. For each of the small flower units, draw two circles, with common center, one circle much smaller than the other. All of the little blossoms connect to one main stem, drawn with your French curve. The leaf outline is a modification of two connected arcs, also drawn with the French curve.

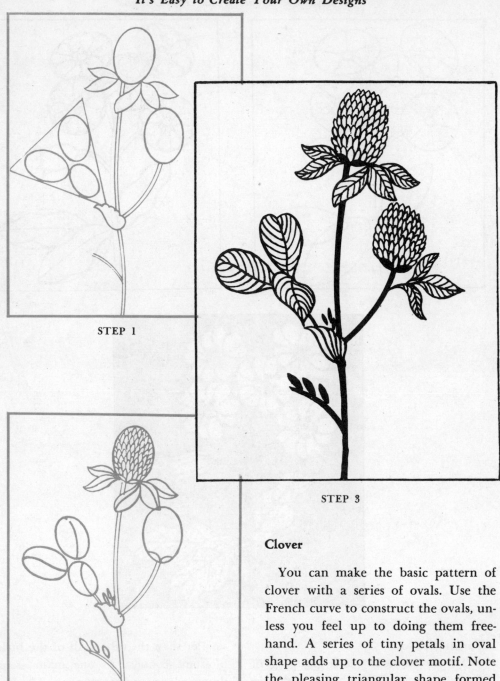

STEP 1

STEP 2

STEP 3

## Clover

You can make the basic pattern of clover with a series of ovals. Use the French curve to construct the ovals, unless you feel up to doing them freehand. A series of tiny petals in oval shape adds up to the clover motif. Note the pleasing triangular shape formed by the leaves to the left of the flower. All leaves and flowers are connected to one common stem.

40

**FLOWERS IN COMBINATION**

Violet, clover, and leaves form a border for a daisy in this arrangement of flowers
suitable for decorating a dish, tray, or other round object.

## A Design of Several Flowers

Design elements that are similar go well together. Try combining several flowers in one design, and you will be astonished at the effective results you can achieve. If, for example, you want to ornament a dish or the inside of a wooden bowl, you might select the daisy as a central theme. Encircle it with an arc of flowers—violet, clover and leaves form the border motif in the illustration. You can make many effective decorations for any type of surface with the easy-to-draw flowers described in the preceding pages.

41

## HOW TO DRAW BIRDS

Next to flowers, birds rank as favorite design motifs in the folk art of American and European home decorators. The Indians were especially fond of them. Among the various national groups, the eagle is one of the most popular subjects in the world of feathered creatures. The eagle was related intimately to national symbols long before it became the American emblem. It can be used in many striking ways in your decoration.

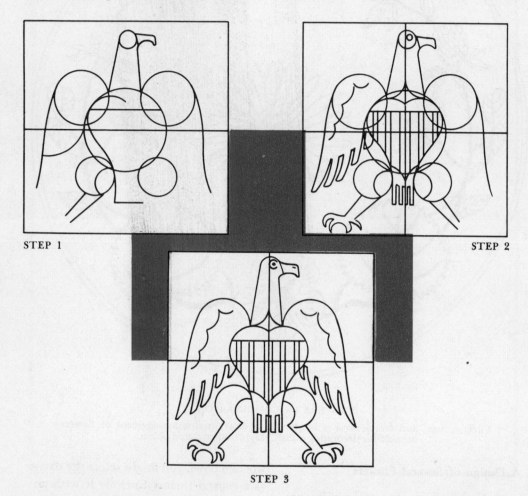

STEP 1

STEP 2

STEP 3

### Eagle

Your compass is the drawing tool for the eagle's body. First draw a large circle to suggest the body. Next, cross it with four smaller ones to provide the basic outline for the top of the wings and the upper legs. To make the outline, extend the curve of the two upper circles of the wings. A ruler may be used to draw the neck and legs of the eagle.

42

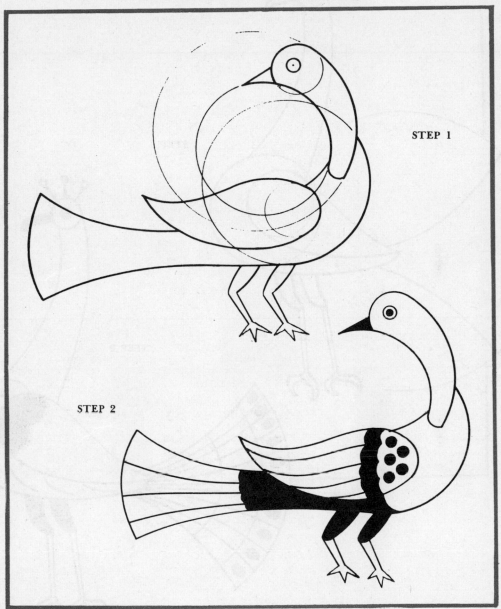

STEP 1

STEP 2

## Dove

The dove—symbol of love and peace as the eagle symbolizes war and strength —is outlined by four circles with your compass. Each circle has a different center. The French curve will serve to guide the arc which forms the tail of the dove. Use it, too, to create the wing. The eye is a tiny circle—make it with the compass.

43

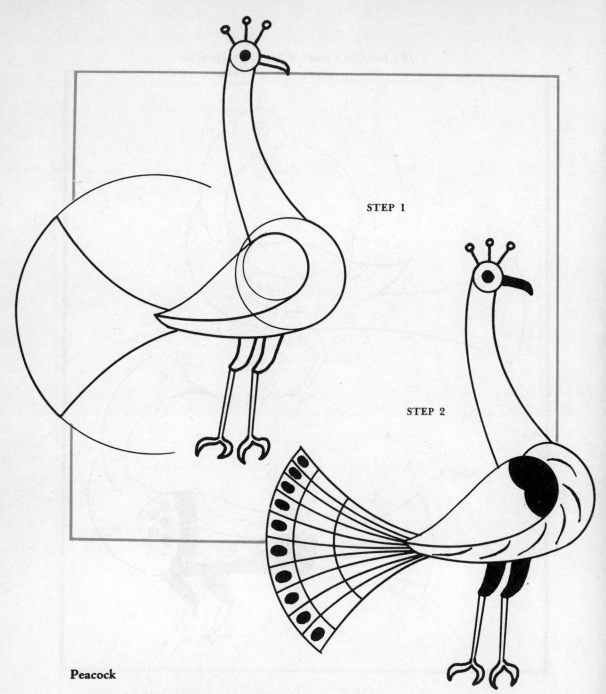

STEP 1

STEP 2

## Peacock

The peacock is another bird popular in the folk art of European peoples. The first step in making it is to draw two circles, one within the other but with different centers. Using the tip of the wing as your center point, draw a larger circle—this gives you the tip of the peacock's tail. You draw the curved neck and tail with the French curve. This instrument will also guide you in making the tail markings.

44

## DRAWING A PIGEON

You can draw the pigeon in the two steps shown, using one circle for the inside of the bird's neck, another for the outside. The French curve will guide you for the other outlines. The pigeon closely resembles the dove.

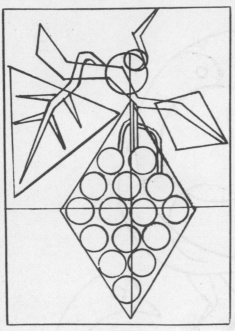

STEP 1

STEP 2

## FRUIT TO YOUR TASTE

A grape cluster is easy to make. First draw a diamond shape. Inside it, with your compass, make a series of small circles, all the same size, as in the illustration. The larger of the leaves fits into a triangle, the smaller into a diamond. Draw the stem in several zigzags, for the most part with a ruler, supplementing it with some free-hand strokes.

In the larger illustration of several fruits, we again have the grape theme. This time you can change the general shape of the grapes by adding one circle to the side to make the design more interesting and less static looking. Triangles outline the leaves, and the

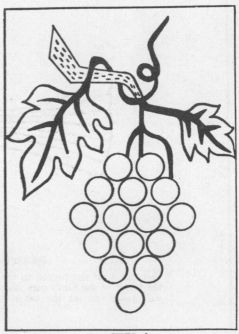

STEP 3

**LEAF DESIGNS**

You can develop leaf designs from simple line motifs, as shown in A;
quartered circle is the basis for paired leaves in B; a divided rectangle for basic leaf in C; circles are the key to the leaf structure in D.

stem is a simple spiral.

The pear is easily drawn with the aid
of the compass — make two unequal
circles touching at one point, and join
them at the sides with two equal curves.

You can represent an apple with just
a circle. Draw the leaves of the pear and

apple with a compass and French curve.

The finished drawing of the fruit
group illustrates how well it looks with
a little shade applied to the general
shape of the objects. The apple, pear,
and grapes may be rearranged in a design of any shape you wish.

47

**PEAR, GRAPE CLUSTER, AND APPLE**

Easy-to-draw triangles and circles provide the frame for drawing the outlines of these fruits.

### FINISHING TOUCHES ON FRUIT

Shading gives the finishing touches to the fruit drawing. In applying these designs to furniture or other objects, use dark paint for the shading.

A

B

C

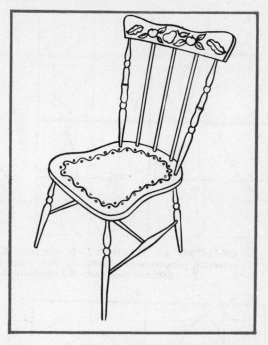

## BORDER AND DESIGN IN USE

Figures of fruits and leaves give a fresh touch to the back of a kitchen chair. Just a wavy line around the seat, with circles or hearts on each side, makes an effective border.

## BORDER DECORATIONS

Border decorations should be in harmony with your design. Fruit, leaves, or interesting lines are very popular. In A, the figures are drawn with pencil and French curve; colors are then filled in. The wavy line in B is drawn with 1-inch flat brush. Make the leaf figures in C with the same aids you use for the fruits and leaves in A. The line in D is done with flat lettering brush, and the heart is added with pencil and French curve, which also provide the line treatments in E.

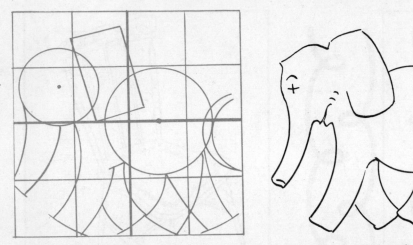

DRAWING AN ELEPHANT—If you rule off squares, it is much easier to copy a correctly proportioned animal, or any other figure for that matter. Two circles of different sizes make the elephant's head, a rectangle the big ear.

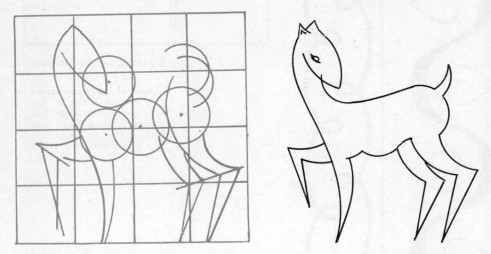

A GAZELLE—Three circles on a slant form the body, a fourth one guides you in placing the head. With a ruler and curve, drawing the graceful legs is no problem.

## ANIMALS WITH LIFE

When you come to more complicated figures like animals, you may find it helpful to use squares as guide lines for your pencil. The smaller the unit of your square, the easier it is to copy the animal figure.

Any size animal can be drawn scaled to the size imposed by your overall space limitations, to fit any piece of furniture or ornamental ware.

All of the animals shown in the accompanying illustrations are drawn with the three simple tools used on the other figures.

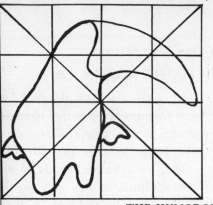 

## THE HUMOROUS TOUCAN BIRD

KID—Two circles govern the proportions of the kid—one for the head, one for the rump. Animals in this light style will be popular in the child's room.

## A FROLICSOME RABBIT
Ovals for head and body are the key to sketching the rabbit.

**THE HUMAN BODY**

The average human being is 7½ heads high, as shown by the circles to the left.

## PEOPLE WITH LIFE

By now you have observed for yourself how much easier it is to create your design motifs, provided you determine the basic elements they are made of. Take, for example, the little angel in the illustration. You can see that the head is a circle and body a single cone with arcs for the arms and wings. A heart — a series of tiny curves — is the mouth, and wavy lines create the hair and dress trim. Applied to a nursery chest or a tile top on a child's play table, the angel would wing its way into any little child's heart.

In creating all of these figures, your main problem is not the basic shape—which follows readily when you are using the mechanical aids — but the proper proportion of the elements.

For example, in the human figures, how large or small are the various parts of the body in comparison to each other?

Fortunately, there are simple rules to follow. In overall height, an average person, erect, is 7½ times the height of the head. The head is measured from top of skull to bottom of chin.

Is your male figure to be larger than the woman? Of course! But proportion holds true in any case. The male head is longer than the woman's—but in each case, the entire body is 7½ times the size of the head.

A woman's arms and legs are shorter, in proportion to the body, than a man's. (From finger tip to toe, the distance is about three heads—elbow to finger tip is two full heads.)

## ANGELS ARE EASY

Anybody can draw a good-looking angel by following these four steps. This little figure will be especially at home on things in the child's room.

## PENNSYLVANIA DUTCH FIGURES

For a quaint old-fashioned touch, try some Pennsylvania Dutch figures. The woman should of course be shorter than the man. Guide-lines are helpful.

55

The body's width, just below the shoulder (at the point of average width) is twice the width of the head. Width between hips is 1½ heads. The width of the female hips is greater than that of a man of the same height—it should equal the width of the chest plus one arm.

The neck and body are 2¾ times the length of the head; the legs are 3¾ times the length of the head. The sitting figure extends four heads from top of skull to the seat. With such rule-of-thumb proportions, and the occasional guidance of the mechanical aids, you should quickly pick up the knack of drawing the human figure.

Do you want to include a child with your adult in a design motif? At three, a child is half the height of an adult; at ten, three-quarters the adult's height. But in each case the proportion of head to overall body height is the same. A tall person may be depicted by increasing the proportion to eight heads in height; a short person, by decreasing to seven heads or slightly less.

## FORMAL AND INFORMAL DESIGNS

Designing does not mean copying from life, necessarily. Is your son to be delighted by a motif of a small boy fishing in a brook on whose bank a tree stands proudly? Make the boy important; let him be bigger in proportion than the tree. The effect will be one of freedom, of lack of limitation such as formal art work imposes. With informal designs, you can have much more fun decorating your home furnishings.

## CHANGING SIZE OF DESIGNS

Often you may find that a design in this book is not of the size necessary to fit properly the space on the object you are decorating. Perhaps you are at a stage at which you prefer to trace the motif from the illustrations in these pages. How can you get the design to the right size?

A simple procedure makes it possible to reach any size you desire, from the figures shown.

Let us say that the elephant in our gallery of animals is just half the size you need. Trace him on your tracing paper. Now, with your ruler, draw over the elephant's figure, at equal distances a series of horizontal and vertical lines, until it is covered with squares—just as shown in the working drawing. Number each of these squares—from left to right, across. Now, on another sheet of paper, draw the same number of squares, each twice the size of those in the elephant design. Number these squares similarly.

Now, from the smaller drawing, copy the portion of the design figure which appears in each square. For example, that part of the elephant figure which appears in Square No. 3 is copied into Square No. 3 of the larger drawing. When all of the squares have been copied, you have the elephant in the larger size.

Reductions in size may be accomplished by reversing this procedure.

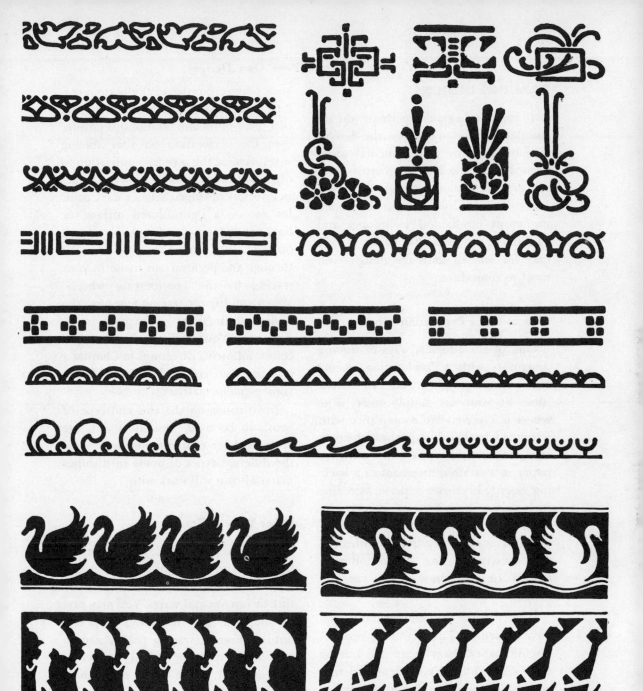

## A VARIETY OF BORDERS

Making your own borders is only a matter of selecting new combinations of elements. They can be as simple as these, which merely illustrate what can be done. New possibilities will present themselves to you constantly.

## TRACING DESIGNS

If you're a beginner, perhaps you are wondering how to start on the decoration of furniture or ornamental wares with designs you have originated yourself or with copies of design forms you fancy. Set your mind at ease. There are numerous mechanical techniques and simplified processes that make it very easy for you to trace the designs you want to reproduce.

### How to Use a Perforating Wheel

One of the simplest ways of tracing designs is with a "perforating wheel" and pounce powder. You can obtain these at your art supply store. The wheel is a pencil-like contrivance with a spiked wheel at the tip where the pencil's lead would be. Rolled on your paper in a straight line, against a backing board, it creates a perforated line such as you have seen on checkbooks, detachable stubs, etc. A control screw makes it possible to adjust the wheel to hold a straight line, or to follow a curved line or draw circles, as you desire.

Simply trace the design motif you have chosen onto a sheet of transparent tracing paper. Now place the tracing over a suitable backing board so that you will not mar a table top, and fasten the tracing securely in place. Go over the design with your "perforating wheel," being careful not to miss any important line element in the design.

Next, secure your outlined tracing to the object to be decorated. Add some of

your pounce powder to the bottom surface of a piece of cotton about the size of a small plum and pounce this powder over the perforation on your tracing sheet. Renew the powder application as often as needed. Pounce powder comes in a variety of colors. Select a dark color for use on a light-colored surface, or light-colored powder for dark-surfaced objects. The pounce powder sifts through the perforations made in your tracing by the "perforating wheel." When you lift the tracing you have the design outlined on your piece to be decorated. You need merely fill in the colors, following directions in Chapter 1 to select your color scheme and obtain your pigment matches.

Instructions on the size and type of brush to be used, and the paint, are given in later chapters which consider the different types of home furnishings materials you will work with.

### Other Ways to Trace

There are, of course, other familiar techniques to follow in tracing designs and transferring them onto your furniture or ornamental wares. You may prefer simply to trace the design in pencil onto a sheet of tracing paper, and to transfer it, with the aid of a sheet of carbon paper, to the object you plan to decorate.

If you are afraid of smudging a light surface with the carbon, you can simply trace the design and then retrace it on its reverse side with a soft pencil. Place the soft-penciled side face down on the object being decorated and redraw the outline on the original side with a hard pencil. You thus transfer a clear-cut line onto the object.

## CUTTING STENCILS

If you are planning extensive border designs, or want to repeat a single design motif on many objects in your home, you will find stencil cutting another valuable short-cut.

For decorating on walls, wood furniture, paper, plastics, pottery and fabrics, small and intricate designs can be made quickly and accurately by the stencil method. An almost limitless number of stencil variations are possible.

The materials you need are: stencil paper (transparent), stencil knife, and (for stenciling on fabrics) a textile pigment.

To transfer your chosen design onto a stencil paper, trace it with a medium hard lead pencil with sharp point. Place the design on a piece of soft board or wallboard; put two pins on the top side of the pattern, and two pins on the left side. Be certain that you attach the pins in line and at right angles to the top edge of the design.

Now place the stencil paper over the design, resting the top and left side of the paper against the pins. Be careful to cut the paper square. You need a separate sheet for every different color, and trace on it only the outlines that will contain that color (see our chapter on decorating fabrics for more details on cutting and using stencils for designs in several colors). After tracing the design onto the stencil paper, remove

the stencil paper and place it over a mirror or other glass surface (a mirror is preferable because it helps bring out the pencil lines more clearly). Now cut along the stencil lines with your stencil knife and remove the paper inside the outlines. Your stencil is now complete.

You have a choice of using stencil paper, tracing linen or aluminum foil for making stencils. While stencil paper will not wear through as many applications as linen, the average home decorator has no great need of such durability, and the greater ease offered by a stencil knife or sharp razor in working with paper more than makes up for the durability of linen.

If you should decide to use tracing linen, you will need a pair of scissors to cut out the paper inside your outlines. With aluminum foil, it is desirable to use pounce powder along with the perforating wheel.

### Applying the Stencil

Even before the stencil is cut, you can be preparing the object to be decorated. In the case of a tin tray, for example, you can finish applying the required two base coats of flat paint—twenty-four hours apart—before you are ready to apply the stencil.

Then the tray is ready for clear varnish. When the varnish has had an hour's drying time, the stencil may be put into position and aluminum bronze powder applied on the areas left uncovered by the stencil. After the varnish has had twenty-four hours' time to dry, the stencil is placed in position and

## APPLYING DECORATIVE TAPE

First paint the object to be decorated. Then mark off pencil guide points along the edges of the areas to be decorated. Select the colors which go with the rest of your decorative plans and apply the tape.

## CUPBOARD MADE GAY BY DESIGNS

A heart is the main feature of this gay design. with flowers growing from it. Small leaves run up and down the sides. Practice combining different figures to create an original design.

# Pennsylvania Dutch Hex Signs

you may start painting on your design. Instructions from this point follow the techniques recommended in the chapter on the type of material being decorated.

## STRIPING A BORDER

One additional short-cut may be suggested for those who plan to frame their decorative design motifs with a striped border.

The task of striping a straight line freehand is tedious, and if you are a beginner it also presents a problem in muscular control.

Fortunately, there is available at many art supply stores an automatic device which simplifies the job of placing a striped border around a tin tray, bureau drawer, or ceramic wares. The device, called a roll-a-paint striper, maintains its control, holding in a fixed position the supply of paint needed to complete the entire striping job and providing mechanical guidance to insure straight lines and an even touch.

## DECALS—A SHORT-CUT

Our main intention in this book is to show you how to do your own designs. But a simple, speedy solution to some decorating problems may be found in the use of decals, available at all sorts of shops. Decal figures are often very attractive; Swedish, Mexican and Pennsylvania Dutch are just a few of the design stylings from which you can make your choice. Different uses are suggested in our last chapter.

Applying the decals is simplicity itself. The decal is dipped in warm water for twenty seconds, then placed on a cloth for a minute. The design is then slid off the backing sheet, and onto the dry surface prepared for decoration. A dry cloth or blotter is used to smooth the decal down and to pick up any excess water, and you can remove air bubbles by rubbing from center to outer edges. The decal dries in a short time, and the design is fixed in decorative position.

In addition to figured motifs, decorative borders are available in decal form, for borders, striping, etc.

Decals are readily removable, by placing a moistened pad of absorbent tissue over them for an hour. Then, using a dull knife or your fingernail, you can easily peel or scrape the decal off.

## DECORATIVE TAPE

A novel way to apply professional-looking stripes with the same skilled effect given by hand striping, though hardly the same degree of originality, is provided by the use of decorative tape. It comes in many colors, including silver, and in several sizes (one-inch, half-inch and quarter-inch widths). Decorative tape automatically gives you good straight-line borders. It is effective on small boxes, wall trim and novelty pieces for temporary decoration. Decals can be used for added interest.

## DESIGNS ALL AROUND YOU

Vivid designs on glassware, a child's tile-topped table, and on other things around you add interest to your home. The old-fashioned piece below suggests what you can accomplish by combining fruit and leaf designs.

Canisters above show a colorful bird and flower pattern painted on a black background.

# CHAPTER 3

# FOLK DESIGNS
# From Around The World

The designs most of us can apply with best effect to the furniture and ornamental ware we desire to decorate are, by and large, those which are least formal. The most colorful and easily adaptable of these are the creations of folk art. They do not require the artistic training called for by more elaborate and rigid formal motifs, and at the same time they bring to home decoration a freshness and gaiety all their own.

Folk or peasant art differs in all countries, but the basic elements are the same. Gay color, some crudity in the shaping of figures, simplicity, and balance in the design—these features are typical. Motifs in geometrical shapes are found in widespread places—even the tribal Indians expressed their inspiration in these mathematical shapes.

In folk art, most of the visible surfaces are covered, but there is no attempt to provide a background for the main design theme. Borders are drawn around the main design to embellish it instead.

For example, if the peasant decorates his daughter's dower chest with a bird bearing a gift of fruit in its beak, he will not attempt to show the trees and other background of a woodland scene. Rather will he surround the central figure with floral designs in an all-over border pattern, balancing the design symmetrically.

## THEMES OF FOLK ART

In all peasant art, the same themes predominate—floral themes being the most popular, with animals, hearts, human figures, birds and mythological figures ranging behind them in favor. But in every place, local interests and experience create certain differences. The human figure is dressed in his native costume in various lands—the

Mexican typified by the sombrero, serape (blanket shawl) and rebozo (a woman's shawl); the Swedish figure by flowered headgear and peasant finery; the Balkan and Turkish by the peculiar footwear, headgear and ornamented dresses. The animal figures are those familiar in each region, and the fictitious beasts of local folklore also differ.

Folk craftsmen and decorators of every time and place, in ornamenting homes and home furnishings and utensils, have drawn extensively upon the symbolism of their religious and mythological lore for their designs.

Here are some symbolic meanings, taken from early art, that in many cases were of wide application:

*Bird looking at its tail:* Fruitfulness

*Pineapple and Acorn:* Symbols of Colonial hospitality

*Double eagle with centered heart:* Symbol of the Holy Roman Empire

*Bird pecking at its breast:* Feeding of young

*Tulips, in groups of three:* Holy Trinity

*Three stamens of lily:* Also denote Holy Trinity

*Star:* A conventionalized pomegranate, the flower symbolizing prosperity and fertility in Solomon's temple.

*Turtledove:* Love and the human spirit

*Peacock:* Resurrection of the dead

*Unicorn:* The guardian of maidenhood

*Blue eye on animal or bird:* The eye of God

## FOLK ART COLORS

Colors differ in various lands according to local taste and tradition. The materials available for producing colors are also a factor in determining which colors will be used. Pennsylvania Dutch colors are often more subdued, and produce more subtle combinations than those found in South American and Scandinavian folk art. On the other hand, favored Hungarian and Czechoslovakian colors will feature deeper reds and blues than the Swedish—and the Hungarians use greens and yellows and golds more freely.

## DESIGNS FOR YOU

In this volume, various typical motits are shown, conveying the inspiration of the differing folk arts which have the greatest influence on our taste in this country today.

The reader may ask: Why use European stylings in decorative design? Why not consider only American themes and treatments?

The answer must be that in today's universality of interest, you are apt to find the closest approach to your individual taste in any of a large number of sources. For all the differences in detail and technique in the world-wide scope of folk art, the appeal of design knows no national boundaries. Any distant source is apt to be a suitable medium for your own self-expression.

American sources are considered along with other folk art examples, so that you have a wide variety to choose from.

64

**BARN WITH HEX SIGNS**
Displayed on this barn are the circular hex signs of the Pennsylvania Dutch—decorative symbols meant to bring good luck.

One reason for the strong emphasis on Pennsylvania Dutch art in this and succeeding chapters—and in contemporary furnishing styles—is that it combines both European and American factors. The traditional European patterns were fitted by conditions of pioneer life into an American mold. In addition, the Pennsylvania Dutch decorative motifs and technique are suitable to a wide variety of furniture stylings, and the design treatments are especially fitted for handling by the beginner.

## WHO ARE THE PENNSYLVANIA DUTCH?

Some confusion exists today over the origin of much early American craftsmanship, due to the fact that many pieces were brought from Europe by early settlers. We can, however, recreate the high points of this early art by examining the many authentic examples of early craftsmanship currently available.

The first German immigrants—lured by no less a person than William Penn himself, who twice journeyed to Germany—came from the area of Crefeld and the Palatinate region of Germany; also Alsace-Lorraine, Switzerland, Silesia, and Saxony, and settled in America around Germantown. When they landed in this country, the British diverted many of them to the Schoharie

**THREE HEX SIGNS**

These designs are of the type the Pennsylvania Dutch painted on their barns. The basic outline is a circle. With compass, ruler, and French curve they may be quickly reproduced.

Valley of New York. Some settled in Maryland, South Carolina and parts of New Jersey. Ultimately, most of them migrated to Pennsylvania. In time, the Quakers feared that they might be outnumbered, and set up restrictions which moved many of these families to the countryside surrounding Philadelphia. By 1775, more than seventy thousand Germans had settled in Pennsylvania.

Although this group represented quite a mixture, the majority were simple and pious folk with a will to succeed in the land of their adoption. These people, unlike others who farmed land in a manner to destroy it and then moved on, built for future generations. They were the first to fence in cattle. They built huge barns with flax-straw thatched roofs that overshadowed the farmhouse itself.

And with their feeling for permanent, substantial homes, they had a desire to ornament both the structure and the furnishings and equipment within. They evolved a striking craftsmanship as they expressed themselves artistically.

## PENNSYLVANIA DUTCH DESIGNS

In choice of design, religious motifs and symbols were highly important to the Pennsylvania Dutch. Among them were Dunkards, Moravians, Mennonites, Labadists, Lutherans, Reformed, Boehmists, Baptists, Quakers, as well as members of the Church of England. Their art and their design motifs were unified into a single "Pennsylvania Dutch" style and color treatment, vary-

### PENNSYLVANIA DUTCH PLATES

Although painted more than a century and a half ago, these designs still retain their charm. The flower on the plate to the left is the ever-popular tulip. *(Courtesy of Philadelphia Museum of Art).*

ing only with the individual craftsman.

Some of the best examples of Pennsylvania Dutch architecture are to be found between the Schuylkill and Susquehanna Rivers outside Philadelphia.

Most of the early objects made by the Pennsylvania Dutch were for use only, without ornament. As living conditions improved, they had time and facilities to devote to the production of decorative patterns, which showed up their homeland origins.

This art was largely a repetition of varied designs and patterns originating from many European sources. These basic themes were continually modified and improved from the standpoint of craftsmanship and skillful execution. Ultimately, the designs were simplified

and expertly adapted to materials native to Pennsylvania. This naturally resulted in the creation of entirely new design styling, which we know today as "Pennsylvania Dutch."

### Hex Signs

Take the "hex" signs, for example. Religious services of some of the more conservative Pennsylvania Dutch sects were held in the barns of the members of the various congregations—a practice still continued — and distinctive symbolic emblems were inscribed on the walls and windows of these barns. These geometrical designs and star-shapes were meant to ward off evil spirits and invoke blessings. Some of

L. ROSS

Plate Design from Montgomery County Pa. 1793

**PEACOCK**

Showing the Pennsylvania Dutch peacock adapted to a modern design.

### The Popular Tulip

them are illustrated in this chapter. They are an important source of our design inspiration today.

The most prominent design featured in the art motifs of these people is the tulip, and it gained extensive favor as a decorative theme in pottery. Doubtless because of the simplicity of the basic outline of this graceful flower, it has been widely copied and adapted in design themes.

The tulip is universally important as a motif in European folk art, because of the wide popularity gained by the flower after it was introduced in Europe in the sixteenth century. It affected political, economic and religious life on the continent in the centuries that followed. At one time it was responsible for a severe depression, the result of widespread speculation in tulip bulb culture. But through all these circumstances the simple outline and strong color of the tulip kept it in first place as a floral design motif in folk art.

### Other Favorite Designs

Besides the tulip, flowers favored for

68

Design From
*Montgomery County Pa.*
1798

## THE DISTILFINK

The mythical distilfink in a popular two-bodied form is shown here combined with a tulip-and-heart theme. This design is modeled after one which dates back to 1798.

design characters by the Pennsylvania Dutch included the lily, rose, daisy, violet, forget-me-not, anemone, fuchsia, carnation and clover.

Along with flowers there was a tremendous fancy for fruit forms, including the apple, pear, grape, pineapple and pomegranate (or love apple). These floral and fruit forms and leaf arrangements served both as central design theme and border decoration.

Nor did the Pennsylvania Dutch neglect birds as subjects of design, par-

ticularly the American eagle, associated as it was with the land of their adoption. (The eagle was also a German state emblem.) The peacock, a "weather prophet" and a religious symbol, was also widely used. Different local birds were reproduced in colorful profusion. These included the pelican, dove, swan, rooster, hen, parrot, heron, scarlet tanager, and the mythical "distilfink," which resembled a robin and was most frequently pictured looking backward.

Animals such as rabbits, deer, lions,

**LEAPING STAG**

This design is taken from an earthenware plate, on which the stag and fuchsias appear in red on a green background.

**PENNSYLVANIA DUTCH
ROOSTER**

This rooster, copied from an original Pennsylvania design, is a highly decorative bird. Here it appears on a china coffee pot. It would look equally attractive on other objects in the home.

horses, lambs and dogs abound in their decorative treatment of glass, tin and pottery objects. The unicorn — the horned horse of mythology—was also popular. So was the leaping stag.

Male and female forms appear in historic portrayals for the most part. Prominent among them is General George Washington on horseback, a favored figure for the ornamentation of hope chests (or dower chests as they were commonly called). Continental soldiers, afoot or on horseback, became a familiar design theme for the Pennsylvania Dutch after Revolutionary times. Partly they commemorate two companies of Pennsylvania Dutch riflemen who answered General Washington's earliest call for troops in 1775, bore the brunt of Valley Forge, and distinguished themselves by their patriotism throughout the war for freedom.

**THEY LIKED FLOWERS**

Flowers appealed to the Pennsylvania Dutch as a feature of their designs. The picture above shows one of their typical decorations, the lily, in a modern treatment you can readily apply in your home.

Other scenes in which human figures abound are interpretations of Bible stories. Naturally, too, many a dower chest bears the stylized figure of a maiden, or of bride and groom.

Pennsylvania Dutch design, like the folk art from which it grew, made liberal use of hearts.

Ultimately, the most skillful of the early Pennsylvania Dutch workers became professionals and leaders in the industrial styling of pottery, weaving, glassmaking, tinsmithing, etc.

In the Pennsylvania Dutch country of this day there are still artisans who produce beautifully styled objects of utilitarian appeal, such as braided rugs, colorful furniture, and distinctively ornamented tinware.

## PENNSYLVANIA DUTCH COLORS

A popular misconception has it that Pennsylvania Dutch color treatments are gaudy or garish, because of their peasant background. But, in point of fact, they are just the opposite. Pennsylvania Dutch shades are soft and delicate, for the early craftsmen used vegetable dyes and earth pigment materials for coloring, which means that the full strength of colors was not available to them. What is more important—you can easily duplicate the exquisite charm of their work by combining the colors shown on the chart in Chapter 1.

Let's see how we apply this color chart in painting Pennsylvania Dutch designs. Ivory No. 10 and Gray No. 18

**PENNSYLVANIA DUTCH PEOPLE**

Birds and flowers add a note of spring to this picture of a man and a maid. The background of the original, a plate, is yellow, with decorations in red and green.

are effective background colors for any combination of the other colors. Pink No. 17 is a suitable background for most of the combinations obtainable with other colors. If there are some other reds and bright colors in the design motif, Pink No. 17 provides an informal note with a design whose spirit is not too serious. When Maroon No. 6 and Olive No. 11, Leaf Green No. 12, or Forest Green No. 13 are used in the decorative design, paint Pink No. 17 in the background for a conservative design arrangement.

We recommend bright or light colors for the design treatment when the background is dark (Dark Brown No. 5, Forest Green No. 13, or Dark Blue No. 15). Any of these three colors makes a suitable background for almost every color on the chart, with the exception of Olive No. 11 or Maroon No. 6.

If you want a bright color in the background, such as Indian Red No. 4, Rose No. 19, Leaf Green No. 12, or Purple-Blue No. 3, it calls for light and dark neutral colors in the decorative design. Among those suitable are Ivory No. 10, Light Yellow No. 9, Buff No. 8, Dark Blue No. 15, and Silver Gray No. 18.

## SWEDISH DESIGN AND COLOR

While every European country — in fact, every area throughout the world— has developed a folk art in decoration of furniture and utensils for the home, the Scandinavian, and in particular the Swedish, peasant décor has been among those most fruitful for modern inspiration.

Swedish decorative design, in general, makes use of the same subjects for motifs that we find in peasant art everywhere: floral stylizations, animals, hearts —and, more commonly than elsewhere, the griffin, the winged horse which in some mythology is half-lion and half-eagle, denoting the combination of strength and speed.

### Art in the Swedish Home

The peasant in the Land of the Midnight Sun, beguiling the time of long winter, gave careful attention to decorating pieces, and applied his flair for ornamentation to textiles, metals, ceramics, glass and woodwork. Each province developed a distinctive decorative style: in one area, geometric patterns predominate, while in the far north country the native animals (horse, reindeer, bear) are most common, along with flowers and the characters of peasant folklore.

The colorful costume of Swedish festivals is particularly distinctive in illustrations on cupboards, drinking vessels, spoons, bowls, spinning wheels and looms, horse collars, sledges, harness and saddles, and chests, bedsteads and other home furnishings.

In a land where wood has been plentiful throughout history, both paintbrush and carving knife serve as tools for the home craftsman's illustrative tastes. Clocks, benches, playthings—everything

**SWEDISH TULIP**
This traditional Swedish tulip-and-petal theme goes well on a modern pitcher.

## SIMPLE SWEDISH BORDERS WITH SUGGESTED COLORS

These eight simple, fun-to-do designs, reproduced on this and the next two pages, depend for their effect, in large measure, upon the use of the brilliant colors and lines typical of Swedish folk art. In each instance it is suggested that the patterns be carried out against a plain white background.

Scroll in vermilion, small circles in blue, flowers alternating, one with black center and yellow petals, the next with yellow center and black petals.

Crossed elements can be vermilion with blue floral tips. Small dots can be blue, daisy heads can be shown with blue petals and yellow centers.

Birds can be drawn with vermilion and yellow outlines and blue eyes and vermilion and green outlines and blue eyes, flower stems can be green, hearts red, petals can be blue and red.

Crowns can be in alternate colors, vermilion and blue, solid color or outline, or all one color. Scroll between crowns can be yellow.

This border can take vermilion, green, and blue in a variety of combinations.

Red tulips with green scrollwork and blue dots will make a typical and easy-to-do Swedish decoration.

Red loops, with blue dots and green diamonds are suggested.

Here is an opportunity to use black for the scroll treatment with vermilion and yellow tulips, with blue leaves and touches of yellow.

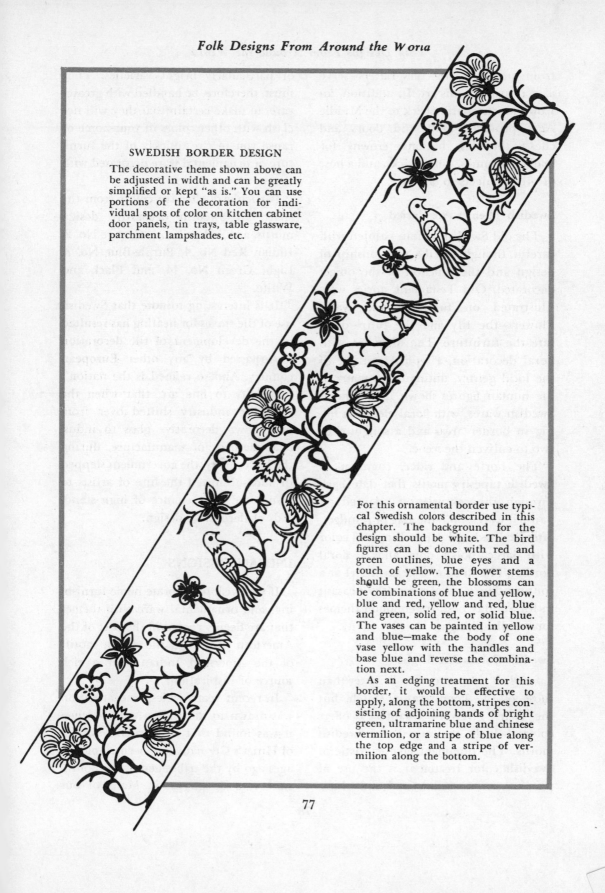

## SWEDISH BORDER DESIGN

The decorative theme shown above can be adjusted in width and can be greatly simplified or kept "as is." You can use portions of the decoration for individual spots of color on kitchen cabinet door panels, tin trays, table glassware, parchment lampshades, etc.

For this ornamental border use typical Swedish colors described in this chapter. The background for the design should be white. The bird figures can be done with red and green outlines, blue eyes and a touch of yellow. The flower stems should be green, the blossoms can be combinations of blue and yellow, blue and red, yellow and red, blue and green, solid red, or solid blue. The vases can be painted in yellow and blue—make the body of one vase yellow with the handles and base blue and reverse the combination next.

As an edging treatment for this border, it would be effective to apply, along the bottom, stripes consisting of adjoining bands of bright green, ultramarine blue and chinese vermilion, or a stripe of blue along the top edge and a stripe of vermilion along the bottom.

from utensils to the very rafters—serve as a canvas for his art. In addition, an iron industry dating back to the Middle Ages provides ironbound doors and chests, buckles, buttons, crowns for bridal costumes, candlesticks, and a host of other objects to decorate.

## Swedish Themes Are Varied

The old Swedish artisan painted with careful thought to the relationship of design and the function of the object decorated. Old Testament stories were illustrated on furniture and walls. Flowers—the lily and the tulip—decorate the furniture. The high hat with floral decoration, a typical costume of the local gentry, distinguishes many of the human figures shown in decorated Swedish wares, with floral elements filling in border areas and a songbird or two to enliven the scene.

The horse and rider, common in Swedish tapestry motifs that date back through the centuries, is adapted on painted wares. So is the stag or reindeer, often stylized and painted in solid color with large polka dots and a floral border. The dress of a peasant girl at a country dance, or of a wealthy peasant in his Sunday best, are common themes for Swedish designs.

## Swedish Colors Are Bright

Swedish colors are often brighter than those of the Pennsylvania Dutch, but the chart given in Chapter 1 offers colors which are suited to Swedish motifs. The dominant characteristic of Swedish color treatment is the use of primary colors—yellow, red and blue—of particularly bright varieties. They must, therefore, be handled with greater care, to make certain that they will not clash with other colors in your home or cause you to tire quickly of the furniture or ornamental ware decorated with them.

Particularly effective colors from the chart, in Swedish decorative design motifs, are Yellow No. 1, Orange No. 2, Indian Red No. 4, Purple-Blue No. 3, Light Green No. 14, and Black and White.

It is interesting to note that Swedish use of tile stoves for heating has resulted in the development of tile decoration unsurpassed by any other European country. And so refined is the nation's sensitivity to fine art, that when the glassware industry shifted over from handblown decorative glass to industrial methods of manufacture, during the last century, the government stepped in and subsidized the hire of artists to insure the maintenance of high standards of decorative design.

## INDIAN DESIGNS

If you wish to decorate home furnishings and ornamental ware with themes that are deeply rooted in the past of the American continent, the design motifs of the American Indian offer a rich source of inspiration.

In recent years, widespread attention was drawn to the Indian sources when it was found that the swastika symbol of Hitler's Germany had been employed ages ago by the tribesmen of the Southwest as a design motif. Many of our

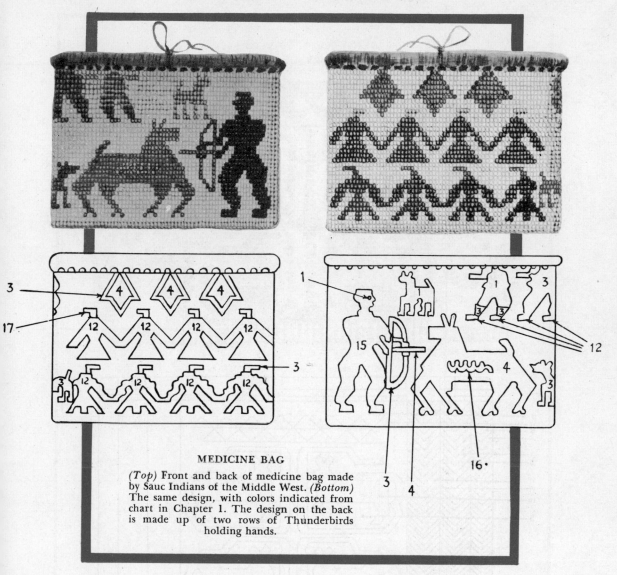

### MEDICINE BAG

*(Top)* Front and back of medicine bag made by Sauc Indians of the Middle West. *(Bottom)* The same design, with colors indicated from chart in Chapter 1. The design on the back is made up of two rows of Thunderbirds holding hands.

public buildings, restaurants, blankets, etc., bore the swastika emblem, and it became necessary to recognize the design for what it was—an Indian "good luck" symbol, rather than the token of Nazi doctrine propagated overseas. The emblem itself has a separate and parallel history dating back to ancient

Greece and beyond, the very word deriving from ancient Sanskrit and meaning "well-being."

The types of decoration and color used by the Indians varied from tribe to tribe. Most of the decorations came from natural forms—animal, bird, floral—and were presented in simplified form,

## THE UNDERWATER MONSTER

*(Top)* The underwater monster, a mystic symbol, is represented on this medicine bag of the Mosquawkie Indians of Iowa. *(Bottom)* A diagram of the same design, with colors indicated from chart in Chapter 1.

DESIGNS FROM NEW MEXICO

These strikingly modern designs of a man, a fish, and several animals are almost a thousand years old. They are taken from pottery made by the Indians of New Mexico. You can easily trace them for use in your own decorations.

with the fewest lines and colors possible. The symbolism attached to these motifs changed with the passage of the centuries.

In the decorations of teepee skins and of the rawhide warriors' shield, the horse was a dominant feature of the design motif. The inner lining of skins for the teepee, serving as a windbreak, the Indian craftsman often decorated with scenes of battles and horse stealing.

Geometric designs favored by the Plains Indians, for example, included squares, rectangles and triangles in various adaptations which symbolized horse tracks, snakes, eagles, hawks, arrowheads, teepees, hills, etc. However, no thoroughgoing general symbol language

81

## BORDERS FOR INDIAN DESIGNS

You can readily adapt the simple border elements on these two pages to a variety of uses in decorative designs. They are creations of the Pueblo Indians.

## INDIAN BIRDS

Indian design is rich in bird forms. They reflect tremendous originality and

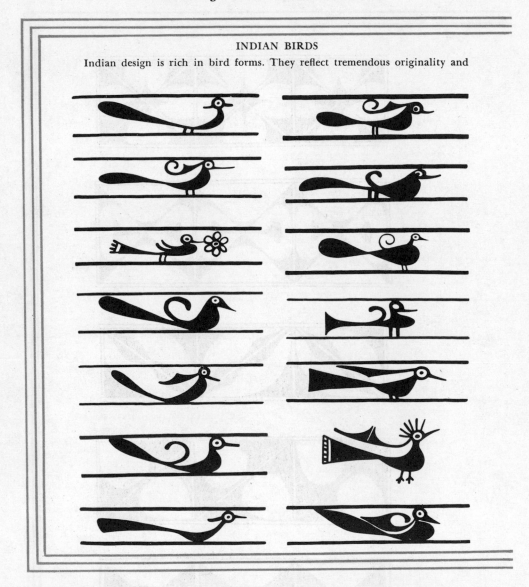

was ever established in decorative motifs. What might mean an arrowhead to one decorator would be a teepee to another.

The typical Indian palette included these colors from our color chart: Yellow No. 1, Maroon No. 6, Light Brown No. 7, Buff No. 8, Ivory No. 10, Pink No. 17. It contained bright purple, green, red, black, white, and other colors as well.

Colors had special meanings for the Red Man. The following color symbolism grew up among the Plains

scope of imagination within traditional patterns. These designs are suitable for over-all design treatments, the simpler birds being particularly good for borders.

Indians, for example:

> *White:* Snow, winter, consecrated objects of nature
>
> *Blue:* Sky, clouds, wind, the west, thunder, water, moon, daytime, the killing of enemies, victory
>
> *Red:* Wounds, sunset, thunder, forms of plant life, hospitality

While the Indian motif represents an American background that is "purer" in its origin, in this book we have subordinated it to the Pennsylvania Dutch because it is more rigid and formalized, and represents a greater problem to the beginner. Indian decorations, further-

**SPEARING THE FISH**

Here is an effective example of the use of distortion in folk art. The fish is almost as large as the boat and the men in it. This design, or a modern version of it, should please a fisherman.

**SERPENTS**

These serpents adorned an old Indian vase, and are still excellent decorative figures for a new one.

more, are less suitable to all periods of furniture styling.

## NEW ENGLAND SEA CHESTS

The home decorator will find rich inspiration in the work of the seafaring men of New England. These seamen of a century ago made models of their ships, carved whalebone and shark teeth in curious designs, and built inlaid boxes and tables, but their chief pride and joy was their sea chests.

These chests were smaller than, say, the dower chests with which a Pennsylvania Dutchman endowed his marriageable daughter. Attractively made out of seasoned pine for the most part, the sea chests were artistically decorated with scenes of seafaring life. The whaling shipmaster operating out of New Bedford sometimes illustrated his chest with whales spouting or diving, sometimes with lighthouses or reproductions of his

**OLD SEA CHEST**

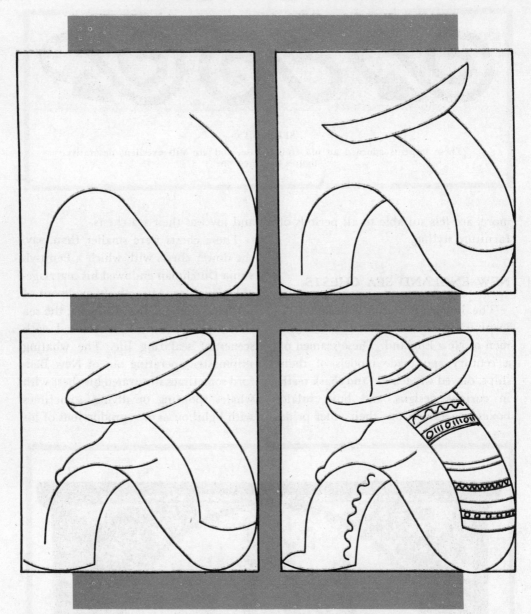

## DRAWING A MEXICAN FIGURE

Illustrating how you can put together a lively, imaginative Mexican figure from the simple basic lines described in Chapter 2. The fundamental line in this figure is the *S*-shape, inverted. Built upon this are the other elements of the Mexican figure during siesta, with curved lines—easily controlled with use of a French curve, if you so desire—as the means of completing the motif.

ships, with the figurehead which proudly adorned the bow of his vessel, or with other noteworthy things he encountered.

Some of these chests were treated with extreme simplicity, so that you will not have too much trouble reproducing the designs on them, either whole or in part.

## MEXICAN MOTIFS

More and more, Americans are turning to the lands "south of the border" for designs and color combinations they can use to decorate furniture or ornamental ware in a personalized treatment.

Actually, great differences exist in the design themes and the application of color in various Latin-American countries. In many, the Spanish influence is dominant, leavened by the folklore and folk crafts of native Indian populations. In others, the Indian theme overshadows all the rest.

Mexican art has had the greatest impact on our own use of folk styling in decoration and in dress. The Spanish influence is strong, with overtones of Indian taste. Mexican colors are Nos. 1, 2, 3, 12, and 16, as shown on our color chart in Chapter 1, and lots of white and black, also dark and bright purple. Americans find Mexican colors less difficult to live with than some other peas-

**MEXICAN MAN AND WOMAN**

Showing a modern treatment of a Mexican woman and a man wearing a serape. The lines have been reduced to essentials. Gay colors belong on this one.

ant art color treatments, because some of the colors are light in value and some dark, providing variety and change of pace.

A typical Mexican design theme is the sombrero, with a cream background favored and bright colors woven into the design. Other costume features popular in decorative art are the serape, the Mexican man's blanket shawl, which may combine green and red and black, and the Mexican woman's shawl, called the rebozo. Besides apparel, religious symbols and the elements of daily life furnish typical design motifs. Geometric patterns, some dating from Aztec Indian culture, are also employed, as are stripes and conventionalized flower shapes.

### SOMBREROS ARE DECORATIVE

You can adapt these distinctive Mexican hats to almost any arrangement you please. Here they are shown at an angle, which lends movement to the design.

# CHAPTER 4

# LETTERING
# For Your Designs

In decorating your home furnishings and glassware or pottery pieces, you may want to use lettering as the basic design motif, or as part of a larger design. On a glass tumbler, a jar, or a vase, a monogram or a name is attractive as a decoration. A bookcase, particularly one used in a child's room, lends itself to decoration with an alphabet. Tile table-tops and tile pieces for bathroom walls, too, look good with a lettering design.

Inscriptions can be made to give an informal and personal note to your overall design effect. Particularly effective in this phase of decoration are the inscriptions found on the work of the Pennsylvania Dutch craftsman. Like him, you may wish to affix your mark and the date to your designs; or you may make an inscribed message an important element in your design.

If you live in the suburbs or the country, and have a mailbox by the side of the road, you can use color and lettering style to transform what is usually a cold and often unattractive feature into a decorative, personal element. The family name on a mailbox, in an individual style and appealing colors, will help identify your home and at the same time create an impression regarding your whole way of living. You can probably think of dozens of other ways you can apply good lettering in and around the home.

Simple lettering shapes are easiest to read and therefore are most usable. Then, too, they are not apt to look "dated." Tasteful lettering forms combine satisfactorily with all arrangements of simple, basic design elements. The alphabets we shall show you here have been selected because they have a broad appeal, because they are easiest to produce, and because they are highly adaptable.

Once you are aware of the effective-

## FOR THE CHILD'S ROOM

An educational as well as a practical object, this piece of furniture may be used for toys or books. Both capital and small letters run around the outside, and there is a monogram on top. Paint the letters red, black, and yellow for appeal to a child.

## LETTERS AND FLOWERS

On this Pennsylvania Dutch chest, the owner's name and a date are combined tastefully with flowers on a decorative panel. Note the small insects on each side of the date. *(Courtesy of Philadelphia Museum of Art.)*

## Children's Party Table

Names have been painted on the glasses with water colors. For greater permanence, oil paints should be used (see Chapter 8). Simple decorations on the backs of the chairs are easy to do, if you follow the method explained in Chapter 5.

ness of some of the simpler lettering forms and understand the correct way to produce them, you should be able to use the alphabets shown as source material. They will indicate an approach to any lettering style you prefer. Use them to stimulate your imagination — as models for your own creative efforts— not for the mere purpose of copying.

To become skilled in the use and application of simple, decorative lettering forms, it is of course necessary to observe good lettering forms wherever they occur, and practice making a wide variety of them. Some of the best appear in the advertising pages of magazines.

## HINTS ON LETTERING

All lettering should have character suitable to the materials used and the

**BOOK ENDS WITH INITIALS**

Putting your initials on objects around the home, like these glass book ends, is an easy and attractive way to apply lettering. Chapter 8 tells you how to paint on glass.

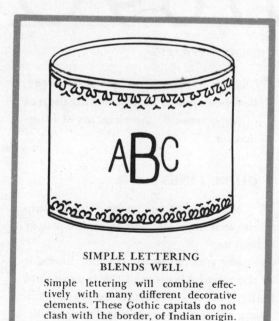

**SIMPLE LETTERING BLENDS WELL**

Simple lettering will combine effectively with many different decorative elements. These Gothic capitals do not clash with the border, of Indian origin. Gold would be attractive on this jar.

purpose for which you intend it.

Avoid distortion or decoration in lettering forms, if legibility is your goal. Lettering for initials or monograms should never be distorted. The basic lettering shapes pictured here retain their simplicity:

The early designers contented themselves with inventing decoration to be applied to the letter form as a thin veneer of ornament. They did not seek to create entirely new letter shapes.

Even though you take no liberties with basic lettering shapes, your lettering need not be dull. To provide variety and interest, your background and lettering colors can be interchanged at will —but be sure to observe the limits described in the chapter entitled "Color Does It."

There is ample pattern interest in a well-made letter used as a background for ornamental figures, animals, flowers, etc., provided they do not distort the letter. A well-made letter—we cannot

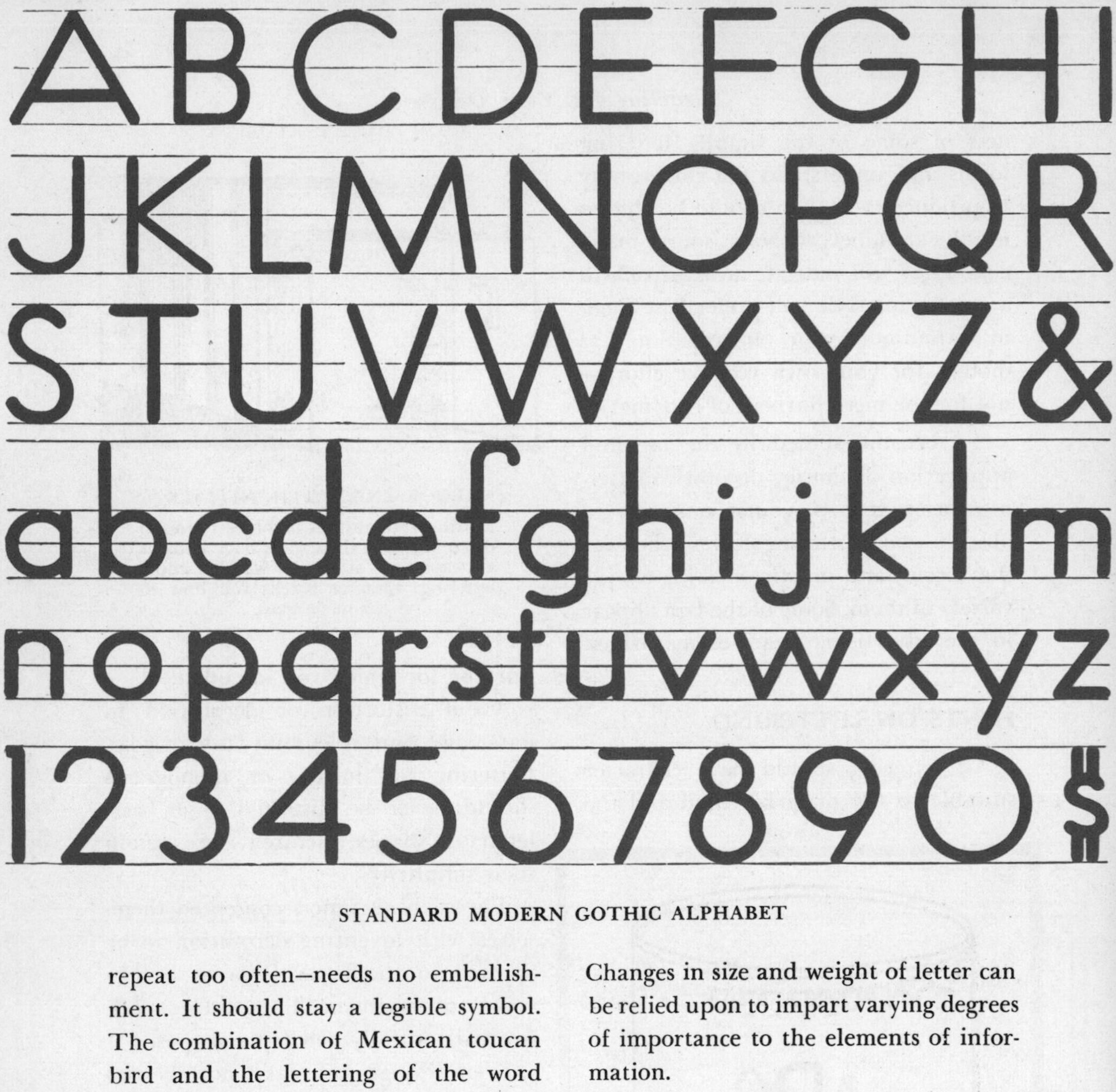

ABCDEFGHI
JKLMNOPQR
STUVWXYZ&
abcdefghijklm
nopqrstuvwxyz
1234567890$

repeat too often—needs no embellishment. It should stay a legible symbol. The combination of Mexican toucan bird and the lettering of the word "Mexico" in our chapter on how to decorate furniture illustrates such a happy combination of design figure and related lettering. The yellow, red and blue colors of the bird's figure are carried out in varicolored letters. The lettering style maintains the spirit of the bird's quaint figure. Yet there is no loss of legibility, and no ornate embellishment, in the style of the lettering.

In general it is best to use only one style of lettering in a single design.

Changes in size and weight of letter can be relied upon to impart varying degrees of importance to the elements of information.

## GUIDE LINES

Most layouts need a base line to keep the lettering level and to insure proper spacing.

For greater detail, parallel lines for the top and bottom of the capitals, and for the length of parts of letters descending below the bottom line, are desirable. Vertical lines can be directed by light pencil marks spaced at proper intervals.

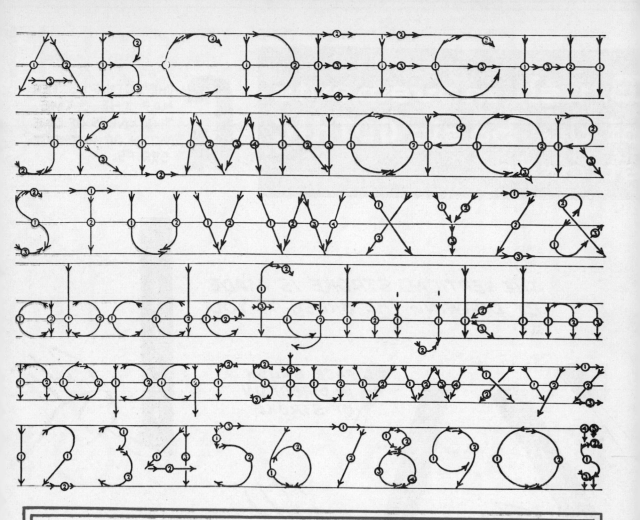

### HOW TO LETTER GOTHIC ALPHABET

This diagram indicates how many strokes for each letter, in which direction they are made, and in which order they are made. All lettering is a combination of a few essentially simple strokes. Note on all curved parts of letters that the strokes overlap slightly. The strokes given are for the beginner; after you are expert, many of them can be eliminated to gain speed. The *C*, for instance, can eventually be made with one stroke.

Spontaneity and freedom of line should not be spoiled by too little freedom of lettering, by too many mechanical controls. Lettering can be as interesting and as decorative as the imagination of the letterer permits.

Don't think of guide lines as a precaution meant only for the amateur or the unaccomplished letterer. Many of the most experienced professionals use them for all work.

# Brush movements of the basic GOTHIC strokes

**G** THE GOTHIC LETTER HAS THE SAME THICKNESS OF LINE WITH OR WITHOUT SERIFS.

THE VERTICAL STROKE IS MADE BY DRAWING THE BRUSH TO YOU.

FACE BRUSH IN DIRECTION OF STROKE

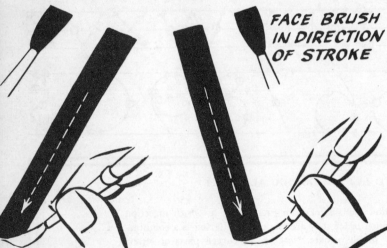

THESE SLANTING STROKES ARE ALSO MADE BY DRAWING THE BRUSH TO YOU.

NOTICE THAT THE FINGER POSITION ON THE BRUSH IS THE SAME ON ALL THE STRAIGHT STROKES.

THE HORIZONTAL STROKE IS MADE BY DRAWING THE BRUSH FROM LEFT TO RIGHT.

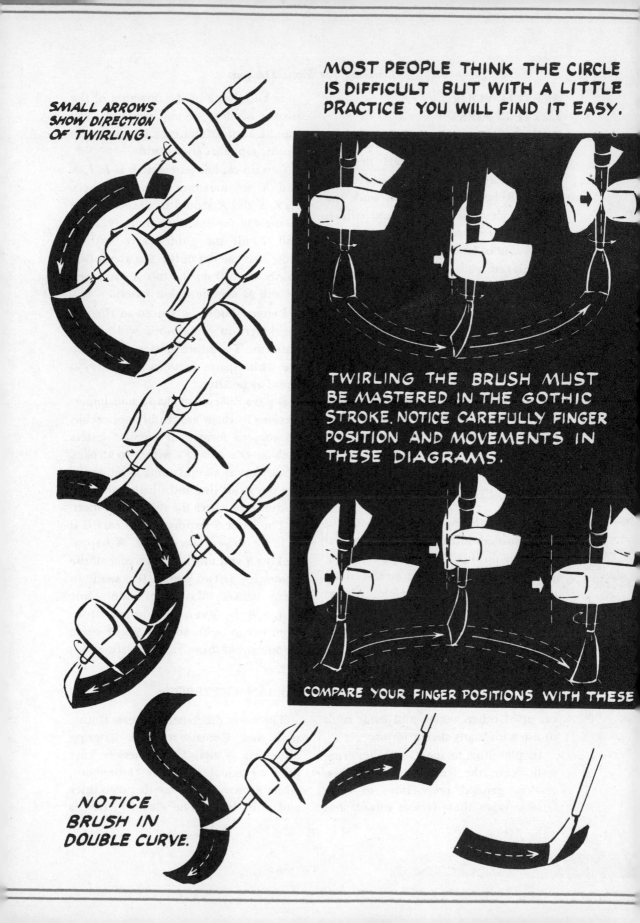

SMALL ARROWS
SHOW DIRECTION
OF TWIRLING.

MOST PEOPLE THINK THE CIRCLE
IS DIFFICULT BUT WITH A LITTLE
PRACTICE YOU WILL FIND IT EASY.

TWIRLING THE BRUSH MUST
BE MASTERED IN THE GOTHIC
STROKE. NOTICE CAREFULLY FINGER
POSITION AND MOVEMENTS IN
THESE DIAGRAMS.

COMPARE YOUR FINGER POSITIONS WITH THESE

NOTICE
BRUSH IN
DOUBLE CURVE.

## SKETCH YOUR LETTERS FIRST

First pencil in the letters or numerals, using a blunt rounded 2H drawing pencil. Hold it well down toward the point. Relax. In all of this work the importance of a relaxed hand (which implies a relaxed arm and a relaxed body) cannot be overstressed. When you are relaxed, your control will be much better.

When the pencil sketching of your lettering and numerals is completed, go over it with brush and paint. A ⅛-inch red sable brush will give you best results.

Make all your strokes strictly in line with the guide lines you have established and be sure to keep your lettering strokes uniform.

## GOTHIC LETTERING STYLE

Gothic letters have the same width of line throughout. Make the vertical stroke by pulling the brush toward you. To make the horizontal stroke, draw the brush from left to right. Always remember to face the brush in the direction of the stroke.

The stems of single-stroke Gothic style shown are made with a freehand stroke of the pen. This lettering can be readily and rapidly made, either vertical or at other angles, and lends itself to use with many design forms.

In planning to use Gothic lettering style, learn the basic shape first; then observe general proportions of these letters. With these factors solved, and your knowledge of the direction of the strokes needed for making them, you should acquire mastery of lettering in Gothic alphabet style readily.

Certain capital letters such as *L, I, N* and *K* are narrower than the others. *X, Z, E* and *K* should be drawn smaller at the top for eye interest. *Y, H, X, A* and *T* fill the guide-square outline. Note that the bar of the *A* is about two-thirds down from the top of the letter. *W* and *M* are the widest letters.

Letters should be spaced so that all the letters in every word will appear uniform. To insure uniformity, make the white spaces between the letters as equal as possible.

*O*'s are difficult to shape, and imperfections in them are readily noticeable. Be sure to form your circular letters such as *O*'s and *Q*'s with two strokes. These letters should come a bit above the top guide line and a little below the bottom one where the two strokes meet.

The letter *S* requires much care if it is to be drawn successfully. A happy-looking *S* will touch the last edge of the guide line at two points. It is made in three strokes. Make the middle line first, add the lower curve in one stroke from left to right, and the upper curve in one stroke from right to left.

## ROMAN LETTERS

The basic difference between Gothic style and Roman style of lettering alphabets is that Gothic letters have lines of equal thickness throughout, while Roman letters vary between thick and thin lines. The Gothic letter is

## VARIATIONS OF STANDARD GOTHIC

Use the upper alphabet where you desire a feeling of weight. The lower alphabet imparts grace and affords you large light areas of lettering when you want them.

# Brush movements of the basic ROMAN strokes

# R
THE ROMAN LETTER HAS THE THICK AND THIN LINE. IT ALSO IS MADE WITH OR WITHOUT SERIFS.

IN THE GOTHIC STROKE THE BRUSH IS TWIRLED. IN THE ROMAN STROKE THE BRUSH IS KEPT IN A FIXED POSITION. IT IS NOT TWIRLED.

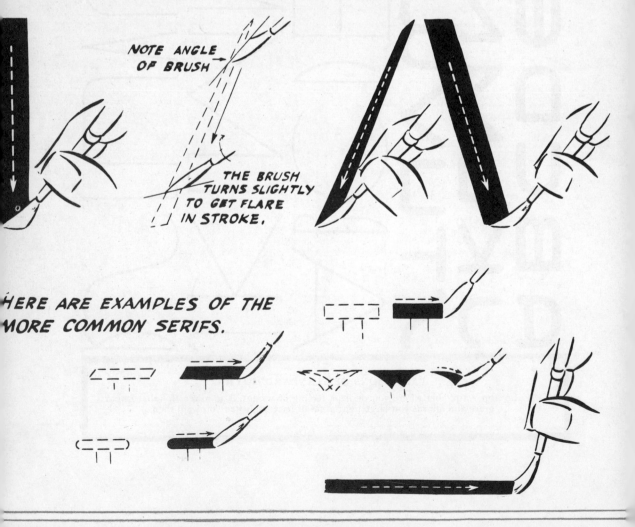

NOTE ANGLE OF BRUSH

THE BRUSH TURNS SLIGHTLY TO GET FLARE IN STROKE.

HERE ARE EXAMPLES OF THE MORE COMMON SERIFS.

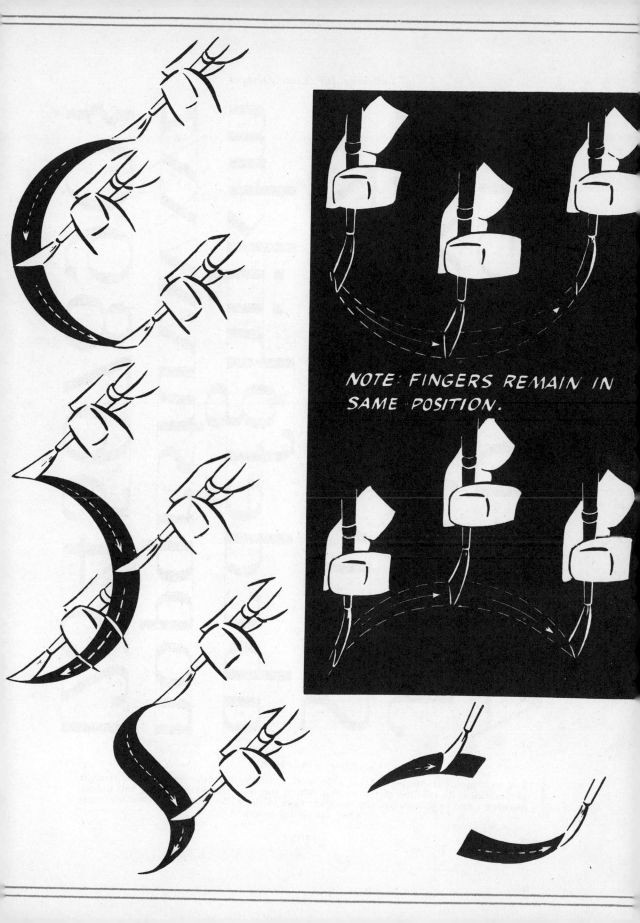

NOTE: FINGERS REMAIN IN SAME POSITION.

ABCDEFGHI
JKLMNOPQR
STUVWXYZ&
abcdefghijklm
nopqrstuvwxyz
1234567890$

## ROMAN ALPHABET

You can produce lettering of this style most satisfactorily with the pen held straight, perpendicular to the line of the writing. When you copy this lettering, you will quickly discover a few variations, like the two slant lines of the *A*, for example. Follow the stroke chart for Gothic letters.

# *Big, bad, bold!*

## ..AND BLEARYEYED

### BOLD SCRIPT

Script lettering can be light or bold. Use one style of lettering in a design, departing from this rule only for some special purpose like contrast, as in the example shown.

made by twirling the brush on curved letters, to maintain even thickness of line; the Roman letter is made by holding the brush firmly at all times.

Both Gothic and Roman letters are made either with or without serifs (the small lines used to finish off the main strokes of letters). As previously indicated, however, you will do well to avoid such curlicues in your decorative lettering.

## NUMERALS

Here are some hints to bear in mind when forming numerals:

Zero differs from the *O* in shape. It is elliptical, not a perfect circle. Care should be exercised in making 3's, as they are easily mistaken for 5's if carelessly drawn.

The other numerals allow you more freedom and scope in perfecting a treatment to suit your taste, as there is little danger that any other pair of numerals may be similarly confused.

### NUMBERS ARE DECORATIVE
Numbers have decorative value, too, like this 8 on a glass. You might use your address, lucky numbers, or, for a child, the number of the last birthday he has reached.

## SCRIPT LETTERING

Script lettering permits greater freedom. In script lettering the possibilities are as varied as the styles of handwriting. The brush strokes follow the easy, flowing pattern of your handwriting. Script style lettering has grown exceedingly popular because it provides individuality and is relatively simple to produce. It is made with the regulation pointed red sable brush in a size to meet the width requirements of the lettering you plan. The width of the strokes is controlled by the pressure on the brush. Press down for a broad line and gradually lift up until only the extreme tip of the brush is touching the surface, to produce a fine line.

## A SIMPLIFIED ALPHABET

For the reader who desires to avoid the use of freehand brush work and the set styles of tracing or of stencil work, we have designed a simplified alphabet anyone can reproduce with just a compass and a ruler. It has been tried with striking effect, on doorplates, on decorated chests, on household utensils, and other articles.

To make the letters larger or smaller, simply change the radius of your compass circle and the length of ruled lines. Letter-spacing presents no problem.

This alphabet takes color beautifully. The black bands shown in the illustration make it easy for you to use a two-color treatment for each letter and numeral. For color combinations, consult the chart and rules of color contrast in Chapter 1.

If you desire a three-color combination to embellish the lettering and set it off against the background colors, all you need do is draw an outline for each of these letters.

## STENCIL LETTERING

For those who wish to use lettering in its easiest form, a lettering guide available at art supply stores and hobby craft shops will furnish a ready solution.

One such guide offers letters on a card with perforations, which permit you to remove each letter quickly and to place it on your decorated piece for speedy copying in outline form. The lettering style is simple enough, and sufficiently informal to be appropriate for most uses.

The prepared stencil lettering guide is so easily used that there is little reason for the amateur to regard lettering as an unattainable feature in design motifs.

Simply rule a guide line for the lettering on your tracing sheet. Place your lettering guide card so that the guide line runs through the center of the indicator holes which will be found over the letters on the card. These indicator holes are also in position to indicate the proper spacing between letters, solving what is often a ticklish problem for the amateur letterer. Use a stiff round bristle brush for applying the paint through stencils. Very little paint is needed. Be sure to wipe the brush often to remove any excess.

Or, if you desire, you may make your own stencil alphabet in any size. Men in service, for example, carved their

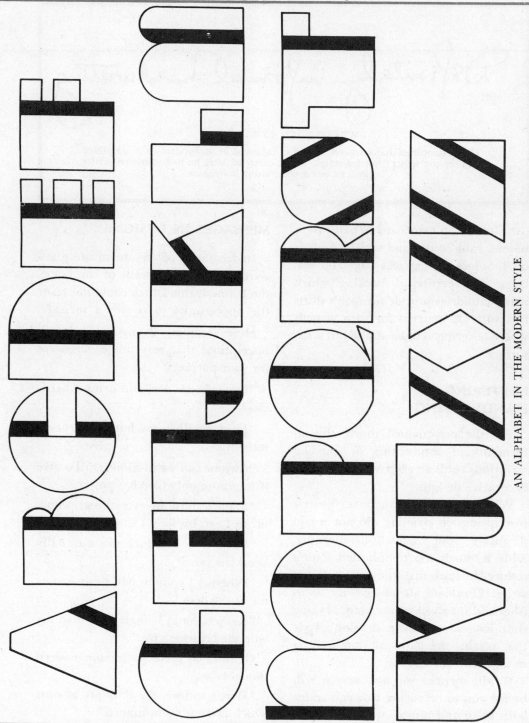

AN ALPHABET IN THE MODERN STYLE

This striking alphabet is easy to make. All you need is a pencil, compass, ruler, and the flat tip of a lettering brush. You are not restricted to black for the wide separation bands—any contrasting color will do. Nor need you keep the black outline showing around around the edges of the letters. You will find it easier to run your color to the very edge of the letter, covering the outline.

*Definitely informal handwriting*

WRITE YOUR LETTERING

This example of handwritten lettering, informal as it appears, is a simplified
form of the writer's normal script. It was executed after he had rewritten it fifty
times or more, eliminating flourishes.

own stencils in cardboard to paint their names, rank, outfit and serial numbers on foot-lockers, barracks bags and sea-bags. The cardboard backing which many laundries provide for men's shirts is a suitable material for such stencils where lettering is to be applied to a flat surface.

## LETTERING IN HANDWRITING

For the personalized touch, the informality of handwriting in your inscriptions lends an effective note to your decorative designs.

When you attempt manuscript-style inscriptions in painting, do not try to duplicate your normal handwriting. This is much too complicated a procedure. Instead, first study the way you write. Eliminate all unnecessary flourishes and involved mannerisms. Making simplicity your keynote, develop a style that retains the flavor of your writing in a general way.

It will surprise you how easy it will be for you to reproduce this new script with paint and brush.

## MESSAGES IN DESIGNS

In decorating pottery, furniture, glassware, and the very walls of the home, the Pennsylvania Dutch could not resist the opportunity to convey a message.

Here are some Pennsylvania Dutch inscriptions that may prove suggestive for your purposes:

"I say what is true and drink what is clear."

"Jesus, dwell in my house and never leave it."

"Anyone can paint a flower. To give it fragrance only God has power."

"I am a bird in everything; whose bread I eat, his song I sing."

"Good and bad luck are our daily breakfast fare."

"Whether I go in or out, death awaits me at the door."

"Rather would I single live, than my wife the breeches give."

Or you may prefer such more modern thoughts as:

"Here's to love, the only fire against which there is no insurance."

## MONOGRAMS

You can create monograms in many different styles and use them on a great variety of objects. Only a few approaches to monogram combinations are suggested here. The top row shows four ways of using *GS*. In the bottom row, a large capital is combined with smaller capitals and small letters. Try reversing the values for a new pattern.

**ALL-OVER MONOGRAM PATTERN**

Monograms repeated over an area make an interesting pattern. This would
be particularly suitable for a tile surface.

If a task is once begun

never leave it till it's done

be the labor great or small

do it well or not at all...

## PROVERB IN A DESIGN

Proverbs or messages may be made a part of your decorative designs. With a border around it and attractive color used in your lettering, the proverb itself will serve as a design.

"May we love as long as we live and live as long as we love."

"Here's to the land we love and the love we land."

Some such sentiment, in your own spirit and attuned to your design, can lend charm to your handiwork.

## BRUSHES AND PAINTS

For brush-lettering designs, beginners need only one or two round ferruled red sable lettering brushes, but they should use only the best grade.

For your single-stroke lettering, select a brush which has a bristle spread the same as the width of the stroke you want to produce. This will give you letters of even width and will prolong the life of your brush.

## SCRIPT ON FLOWERPOT

The Pennsylvania Dutch artisan has embellished this piece of pottery with her name and address, in addition to a decorative theme tying in with the use of the pot. (*Courtesy of Philadelphia Museum of Art.*)

# *Brush Lettering* materials

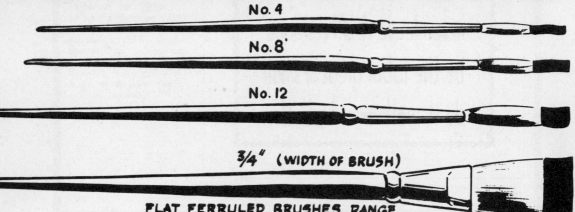

ROUND FERRULED LETTERING BRUSHES RANGE IN SIZE FROM No.2 To No.20

No. 4

No. 8

No. 12

3/4" (WIDTH OF BRUSH)

FLAT FERRULED BRUSHES RANGE
IN SIZE FROM 1/8" TO ABOUT 2" WIDTHS

Especially prepared paints for lettering purposes are now available at sign painters' supply shops. These paints have excellent covering properties, are of the right consistency for lettering, and have a desirable creamy texture.

**How to Hold the Brush**

The brush should be held at right angles to the surface to be lettered. A two-finger hold (thumb and first finger) allows freedom and better contact. The brush should be held on the metal ferrule. Strokes should be applied with a gentle and even pressure.

It is important to learn to work the whole arm with each stroke. Do not tense your grip on the brush. Hold it easily and roll the brush between your fingers as required to make the various stroke motions. Rolling the brush gives you lines of uniform width on curved letters.

Good lettering is the result of care and practice. You should start—using, perhaps, a supply of old newspapers—by brushing in straight parallel lines till you have this element of lettering technique in full control; then work over each of the other elements listed above, until you are confident of your strokes and are ready to apply lettering designs with assurance. It was the great pianist Paderewski who said of practice, "If I miss a day's practice, I notice it; three days, my friends see it; three weeks, and all the world knows it."

110

# How to hold the Brush

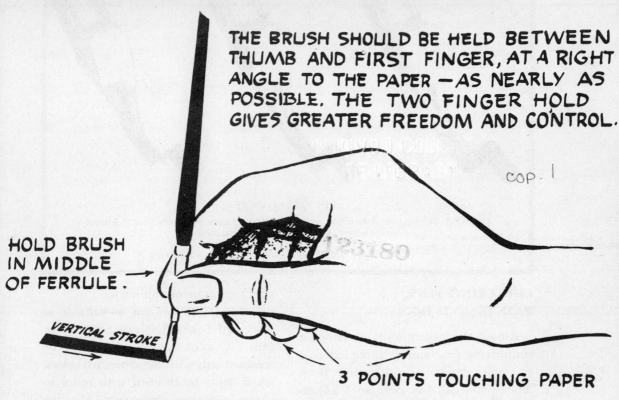

THE BRUSH SHOULD BE HELD BETWEEN THUMB AND FIRST FINGER, AT A RIGHT ANGLE TO THE PAPER — AS NEARLY AS POSSIBLE. THE TWO FINGER HOLD GIVES GREATER FREEDOM AND CONTROL.

HOLD BRUSH IN MIDDLE OF FERRULE.

VERTICAL STROKE

3 POINTS TOUCHING PAPER

GENTLE, EVEN PRESSURE WILL GIVE THE BEST STROKE. THIS IS NOT A FINGER MOVEMENT. THE WHOLE ARM MOVES WITH THE STROKE.

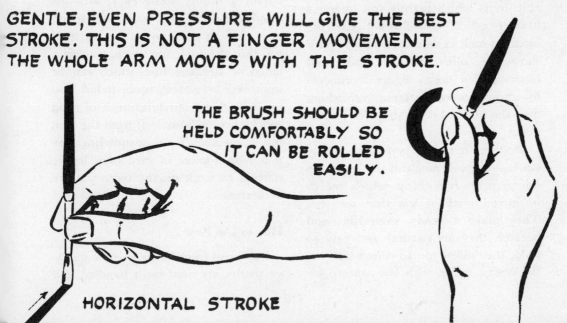

THE BRUSH SHOULD BE HELD COMFORTABLY SO IT CAN BE ROLLED EASILY.

HORIZONTAL STROKE

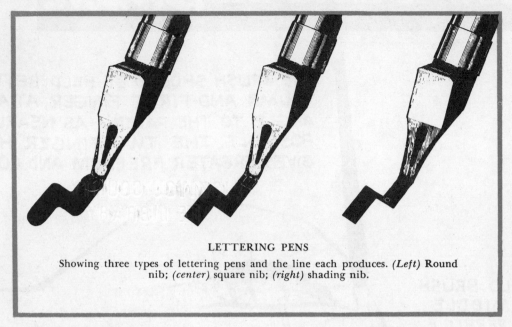

**LETTERING PENS**

Showing three types of lettering pens and the line each produces. *(Left)* **Round** nib; *(center)* square nib; *(right)* shading nib.

## LETTERING PENS, PAINTS AND INKS

Among the modern tools available for simplifying your work in using lettering in your designs are lettering pens. Today you can buy pens with adjustable feeds which permit you to use a heavier-bodied, slow-flowing coloring medium such as show-card colors. With show-card colors you can apply both lettering and design figure treatments to smooth wood surfaces, varnishing over the finished decoration for permanence.

Modern lettering pens save many strokes over a brush, and the letters do not require retouching—which means improved work in less time for you. They make a steady, even line, and because they are natural and easy to hold, they allow you to concentrate on the design figure, with less concern for your technique of application.

Colored inks are not as suitable as show-card colors, but can be used for tints. A solid, opaque line can be achieved only with the show-card colors, which must be thinned with water to obtain a proper consistency. Mix the show-card color with water in a spoon or on a clean dish—not in the bottle. If you thin the color too much, you get a faded or streaked line—which can be improved by adding more paint. You can tell when your mixture is of good consistency—it flows well from the pen, but leaves a solid and opaque line. Try it out on a piece of cardboard before starting to work on the piece you are decorating.

### How to Use Pens

Pens with round nibs give the quickest results, are most easily handled, and

# Merry Christmas...

## AN OLD-FASHIONED TOUCH

"Text" lettering in this simplified version is well adapted for use in designs with an old-time flavor.

are best adapted to modern styles of lettering. When using a reservoir pen, dip it deeply enough to fill the reservoir with coloring material—but do so slowly and gently.

In dipping the lettering pen, avoid inserting it too deeply in the container for coloring material. The sediment in the color settles to the bottom and will eventually clog the point. In addition, if you jam the point against the bottom of the container, it may be thrown out of position. A good procedure is to use a small brush or glass dropper to fill the pen.

To avoid blots, before you place the pen on the surface to be decorated, get rid of the surplus color. After filling the pen with color, touch it against the underside of the container.

Rest the pen in place on the surface of the decorated object at the beginning and end of each stroke, to assure a sharp finish to each end of your line. Hold the pen as easily as you would an ordinary pencil—sit erect as you work, so the weight of your body is not forced on your stroke.

For a round-nib pen the holder should point to the right of your shoulder—for a square-nib pen it should point directly at the shoulder. If possible, keep your forearm and wrist on the surface of the object you are decorating, to assure a steady stroke. Press firmly and steadily on your pen, but not too hard. Keep the tip of the nib flat against the surface.

Be careful about cleaning your pen after each use, to assure good results the next time.

It is better to learn one good alphabet thoroughly, for your lettering work, than to half-learn a great many. Do this alphabet over and over in practice, until you can handle both the pen and the lettering style with assurance. Letters of fine simplicity, easy to read, and modern in appearance, are less difficult to do—and at the same time they offer as much scope for originality as any of the old-fashioned lettering styles with curlicues and fancy flourishes.

# abcdefg

# hijklmn

# opqrstu
# s
# vwxyz

## PREFABRICATED ALPHABET

With the use of circular tape cutouts, available in different sizes, and a strip of tape, you can make any of the letter forms shown above. To make an *a*, for example, simply paste the circular form to your work surface; then paste a portion of tape, of suitable length, to the right side of the circular form, and you have the letter as pictured here. All letters can be composed of combinations of circular forms and strips, or of combinations of strips alone. These paste-on tape aids come in a variety of colors, and may be obtained at art supply stores and department stores.

# CHAPTER 5

# DECORATING FURNITURE In Your Style

This chapter might just as well be called "Working Wonders with Furniture." For it's little less than a miracle when in the place of an ugly old wooden box there stands a wonderful bright red toy chest, decorated with yellow balls, gay clowns, and alphabet blocks of many colors. You wave a paintbrush at a dingy chair and its old-fashioned lines and drabness vanish—it is magically changed into a light ivory chair of rare beauty, with delicate pink ribbons running up and down its sides and a motif of Pennsylvania Dutch hearts and birds sparkling on its broader surfaces. Hand-me-down chests and commodes, pieces from second-hand shops and the unpainted wares sections of department stores can be transformed into attractive furniture in your style by the simple application of colors and designs that reflect your taste and personality.

Make it your basic rule in decorating furniture, that your treatment should emphasize the construction of the individual piece. If your taste is for modern furniture styling, there is no point to start with a piece whose basic lines and materials are those of Chippendale, Hepplewhite, and other ornate styles.

## A Paneled Piece

If you have a paneled piece, the panel units deserve dramatization—they cannot really be blended convincingly, so that an observer would fail to note their presence in the construction. Dramatize them, however, in such a way as to relate to your own interests. A lady I know, whose interest in local amateur theatricals is known to all her friends, started with an old cupboard with paneled doors that once bore delicate Chinese figures; the panels have been decorated as the arch of a stage, with a typical swag of curtain painted on the

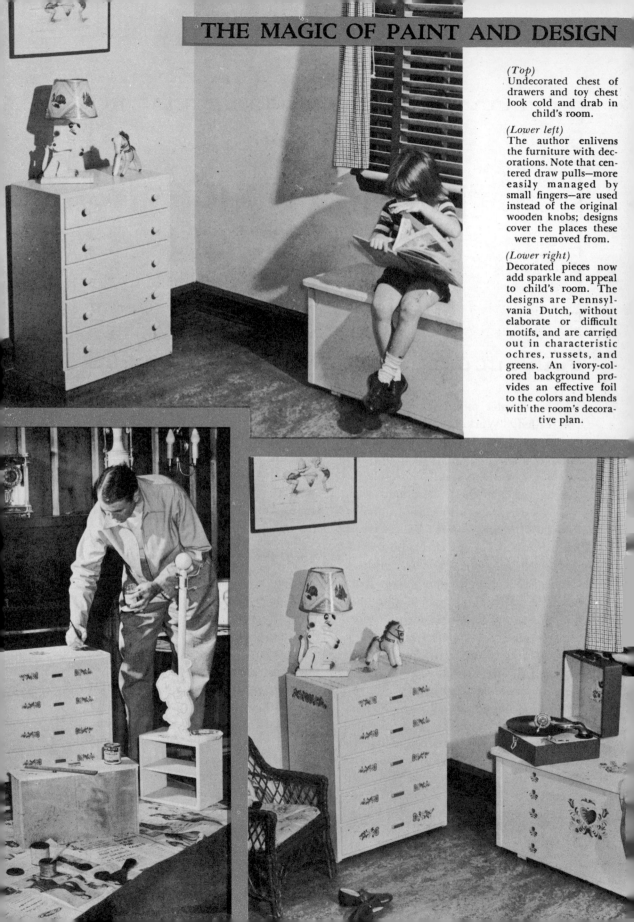

# THE MAGIC OF PAINT AND DESIGN

*(Top)*
Undecorated chest of drawers and toy chest look cold and drab in child's room.

*(Lower left)*
The author enlivens the furniture with decorations. Note that centered draw pulls—more easily managed by small fingers—are used instead of the original wooden knobs; designs cover the places these were removed from.

*(Lower right)*
Decorated pieces now add sparkle and appeal to child's room. The designs are Pennsylvania Dutch, without elaborate or difficult motifs, and are carried out in characteristic ochres, russets, and greens. An ivory-colored background provides an effective foil to the colors and blends with the room's decorative plan.

## DECORATIVE CUTOUTS

Cutouts made of sheeting cork (the kind used for automobile gaskets will do) provide an interesting decorative treatment for a homemade masonite cabinet. The cork material is readily available and easy to work with.

upper area and sides, footlights at the bottom of the panels, and stage scenes occupying the appropriate center area.

## Cork Decorations

In another home, the family's sailboat is given prominent attention in a novel manner. Masonite plaques have been attached by adhesive to the backs of chairs in the playroom, and on the masonite cutout models of the boat (made of thin cork, the kind used in engine gaskets) are in turn attached by adhesive. The gaskets are purchased at auto-supply stores, and similar cork materials may be used by those who prefer such cutouts to color finishes for decoration. (The back, top or sides of bookcases used to establish divisions in dinette or dining room-living room combinations are particularly appropriate for this type of ornamentation; so, too, are nurseries, playrooms, or porches.)

117

**CHEST—BEFORE AND AFTER**

It is generally best to decorate drawers as separate units. This picture shows a treatment suitable for use directly over an unpainted surface or on an enamel finish. Designs are adapted from butterfly illustration in Chapter 2.

### Your Hobbies in Decoration

It would be impossible, of course, to cover the myriad of personal hobbies which may be depicted in your decorative figures to make your furnishings distinctive. Again we should repeat that you will find inspiration as you think over the parts of your daily living which are pleasant, individual, and important to you—and this inspiration will show up in your decorative designs and colors.

Drawers call for ornamentation as separate units. But one family, whose summer Sundays are largely spent in happy fishing parties, has decorated a chest, which is located on their all-weather glass-enclosed porch, with the family fishing from a boat on the upper drawer and all three lines taken at once by a huge "catch" painted on the lowest drawer.

### Consider the Area

Designs must be selected and located on the piece of furniture to be decorated in such a way as to conform to the space to be occupied. Consequently, important designs should be used on pieces of impressive proportions, in important positions in the scheme of your room décor.

## Keep It Simple

In general, it is wise not to clutter up a surface with a whole forest of figures when one or two simple forms will suffice. But one wife, whose husband allows nothing to be thrown away, has restored an old chest from her cluttered attic with just such forest of figures, depicting the many items still stored "upstairs."

With happy humor, she has really made her decorative treatment an expression of the family's personality and problems! Their friends, who know the husband's quirks, enjoy the appro-

**VARYING THE DESIGN**
This chest decorated in the Swedish manner has a different design on each drawer. Varying your designs on one piece creates a refreshing effect of freedom. You must however be careful that designs do not clash in style or color.

**KEEP IT GAY**

Be sure the designs you paint on a child's furniture are gay in theme and color. If he is to enjoy them, they should reflect his preferences. They may serve as a memento of some big event in the child's life — a delightful trip to the zoo or circus.

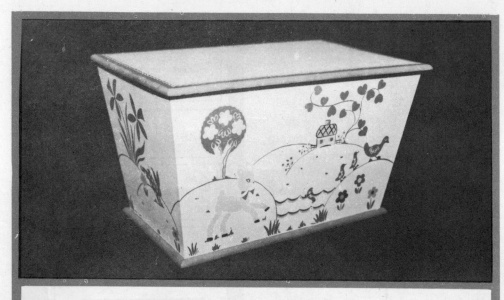

### FARMYARD SCENE

This simple scene, depicting a farmhouse, chickens, and a lamb, makes a fine decoration for a child's toy chest.

### CIRCUS ON A TOY CHEST

The pictures and colors on this exciting-looking toy chest can be repeated elsewhere in the nursery or playroom, giving it a gay childhood theme. Bright colors should be used.

priate ornamentation.

Your possibilities of expression go
beyond the mere use of paints, as indicated by the sailboat decoration on the
chairs described earlier. The variety of
new materials available gives constant
promise of new inspiration. For example, the family mentioned above,
with the joint fondness for fishing, had
an old-fashioned glass-doored cupboard
on the enclosed porch, and has used it
for storage of odds and ends. They
covered the glass panels with opaque
sheets of a new plastic material known

makes the piece into a modern and attractive item of furniture. The iridescent effect of the pearl-essence surface gives beauty of color and depth. And, of course, it is a pleasant reminder of the family hobby!

## BRING IT DOWN FROM THE ATTIC

All the joy of the inventor and the artist belong to the homemaker and the handy husband who can create a usable piece of furniture out of some old relic consigned long ago to some attic—to your attic, or your grandmother's, or the attic of the lady who finally sold the piece to the second-hand dealer.

In truth, the better value today may

**CHILD'S CHEST OF DRAWERS**

One decoration always in place on furniture in a child's room is his name. The lettering can be rough and unconventional—perhaps a copy of the child's own printing or script.

**BACK IN STYLE**

An old-fashioned sewing machine with quaint decorations on its wood and metal parts will lose its forbidding appearance and fit pleasantly into many a room décor.

as irilite, in which a fish-scale surface of the type used in making synthetic pearls is molded. Use of this material over the glass panels serves the double purpose of making the untidy interior shelves of the cabinet invisible to guests and

be found just as often in unfinished furniture available at department stores and furniture shops. But there is a certain adventure and satisfaction in putting an old piece into condition to serve your needs. This satisfaction is sometimes greatest when it involves, in addition to the decoration, adaptation of the piece to an entirely new purpose.

For example, an old-fashioned commode can be converted into a chest suitable for a small space by removing the mirror. A chest of drawers, with shelving added, and plywood back and sides attached to the shelving, can become a kitchen cupboard. Often, in such cases, it is necessary to remove the legs below the bottom drawer, to bring the chest down to work-table height. On the other hand, an old-fashioned bureau can be converted into a dressing table by adding a mirror to the top—with decorated plywood backing.

Among some enthusiasts, indeed, there may be a tendency to get involved in a carpentry job on an old piece unnecessarily, to make the change in function for change's sake alone. Your plan of action depends on whether your primary interest is the fun of making a new piece—or the satisfaction of getting use out of an old piece according to your own pattern of living.

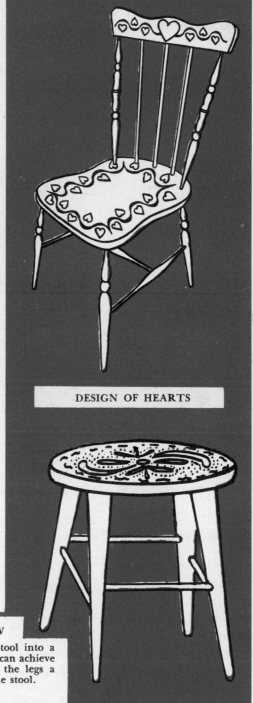

DESIGN OF HEARTS

OLD STOOL MADE NEW

Paint and design transform an old stool into a new one in the Swedish manner. You can achieve an attractive style note by painting the legs a different color from the rest of the stool.

123

**UNPAINTED CHEST—BEFORE AND AFTER**

The finished chest offers a graceful adaptation of the daisy design shown in
Chapter 2. Note how drawer pulls have been worked into the decoration. A simple
border of leaves ornaments the top and sides of the chest.

### New Use for Old Radio

A favorite conversion is to put an old
radio cabinet to new use. The advent of
small table-model radios today has left
many homes with obsolete consoles. By
removing the shelves, and employing a
little carpentry, you can have a storage
cabinet with shelves—a bookcase—a
writing desk.

### Make a Secretary

An old table can be made into a
bright and useful secretary by attaching
an upright piece of plywood to the rear,
and attaching shelves and cubbyholes to
the plywood. A Victorian desk can
become a more modern secretary by
removing the upper section with its
pigeonholes and converting that por-

# Furniture

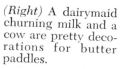

*(Left)* This chest, bookcase, and mirror were outmoded pieces relegated to the attic before Norwegian designs turned them into handsome furniture in the folk art tradition.

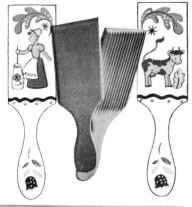

*(Right)* A dairymaid churning milk and a cow are pretty decorations for butter paddles.

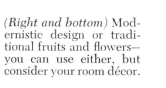

*(Right and bottom)* Modernistic design or traditional fruits and flowers— you can use either, but consider your room décor.

# Designs by Decoupage

You can make many unusual and attractive decorations by a simple method called decoupage. All you do is select and cut out colored illustrations, arrange them pleasingly, and paste them down on a dresser, chest, or other piece. You lacquer them over to preserve them.

## "Antique" Chest

This ancient-looking chest is really quite modern. But its lines are old-fashioned, and the design has been chosen accordingly. For a finish, antiquing or glazing gives a mellow effect.

### DECORATIONS MAKE IT SMALLER

This ample chest is made to appear a trifle less ponderous by the use of a simple decorative border. The border tends to lead the eye away from the outlines of the massive piece, creating the impression that it is no larger than the area enclosed by the border. The central decorations on the drawers and on the top of the chest also distract the eye from its full dimensions. The use of bright colors in the decorations helps this effect.

tion into a hanging whatnot. An ugly chest may be made into a useful bookcase.

**Easy Alterations**

In the field of simpler construction, a board can be bracketed to the wall for a typing desk—or made into a dressing table by hanging a mirror overhead and suspending a ruffled skirt to the floor. Sturdy old picture or mirror frames become trays, with plywood or masonite backing. An ironing board becomes the surface of a coffee table, perhaps with the inverted rockers of a discarded hobbyhorse as legs.

Often the legs of an old table or chest give it a top-heavy or ugly appearance. By removing the legs you improve the appearance and create a more modern size. Often, too, metal drawer handles are both unattractive and a give-away as to the age of a piece; wooden knobs can replace them inoffensively, and can be worked into the design—as flowers, per-

haps—to add a positive touch.

Sometimes the use of color alone can recover for beauty the lines of a piece which is not attractive because of certain shortcomings of design. For example, many a chest is unappealing to the eye because it seems too high for its width and depth. Decorative design treatment which emphasizes horizontal lines and avoids the vertical plane will tend to remedy this effect.

## Use Imagination

Naturally, your ability to create new uses and attractive appearance for outmoded pieces of furniture will depend upon your talent and imagination. You may notice a forlorn-looking piece of furniture—in cellar or attic, or in some location where it is neither attractive nor satisfactory. That fact of observing is the first step.

The second, and more important

**INFORMAL CHEST—
INFORMAL DESIGNS**

So informal are the lines of this old-fashioned chest that to treat it in any but a casual style would make it seem out of character. A happy blend of gay colors and simple designs—each a heart surrounded by flowers—provides a rich appearance.

step, is to visualize the piece in new trappings . . . serving a different purpose in your home. Train your imagination to skip the close association and link up with associations that are further away. So the old radio cabinet will get a new lease on life as a writing desk with book-shelves added.

The design and color plans you produce will excel in boldness, freedom from restraint, and originality, when you permit your imagination to direct your creative work. But remember that the difference between obtaining a reaction from your guests of "That's quaint! Charming!" and a condescending acknowledgment that "It's homemade, isn't it?" will lie in how you apply your decoration.

## CREATING NEW FURNITURE WITHOUT HAMMER OR NAILS

Your wonder-working activities with furniture can be just as creative when they are not strenuous. Without so much as lifting a hammer you can design and build your own pieces. This is simply a matter of bringing ready-made elements together into new combinations. A striking living room table and other pieces, as we are going to show you, may be created inexpensively by this unorthodox method. The only limits are those set up by your own ingenuity. Let usefulness be your first goal. Once you have made the piece, your own taste in decoration can give it color and character.

### A Novel Living Room Table

To make a living room table, we first need to consider the size desired, next the color which will blend best with the surroundings in which the table will appear. Obviously, if you can afford to pay two or three hundred dollars, there is little need for making your own table, unless you're a craftsman at heart. But suppose you can afford to spend only twenty-one dollars? What sort of a table could you find on the open market today? Not very much of a product, we're afraid. Workmanship comes high at present rates. So, let's see what can be accomplished on your own.

Suppose your living room is twenty by twelve feet—then a table size seven by two and a half feet would be about right. There are many ways that a table top of this size can be constructed from planking. However, $3/4$-inch-thick plywood can be purchased, cut in a section to this size. If a more substantial top is desired, a flush plywood door will serve. The plywood can be obtained readily from any lumberyard, and comes in a variety of attractive wood finishes, as do the doors. Birch, walnut, or oak can be attractively stained and finished.

For supports, a couple of sawhorses will do. These can be obtained through most lumberyards and can be cut to any required height. The cost of a plywood top or a flush plywood door is modest. Sanding, staining, and finishing would be the only other cost factors.

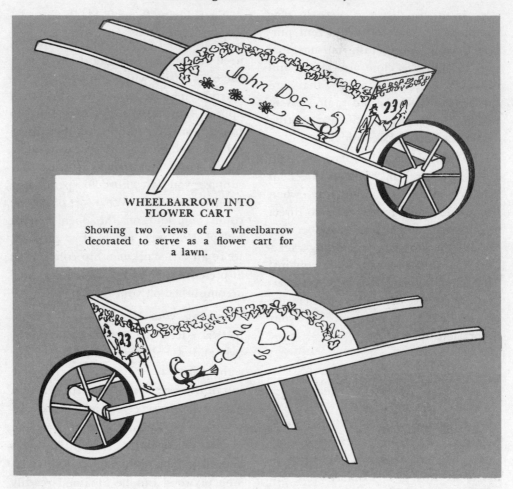

**WHEELBARROW INTO FLOWER CART**

Showing two views of a wheelbarrow decorated to serve as a flower cart for a lawn.

## An Easy Desk to Make

Let's apply to the construction of a desk the same principle of substituting simple materials and ingenuity for costly but uninspired craftsmanship. Reduced to essentials, most desks are nothing but drawers surmounted by a writing surface. You can make an attractive piece just by setting a plywood top across the surface of twin two-drawer files, separated by enough space for your legs. Use design and color to give it personality.

## A Flower Cart for Your Lawn

Suppose you have a wide expanse of lawn in front of your house. You're faced with the problem of giving it a distinctive decoration, but you do not favor the store-bought figures of people and animals that tenant your neighbors' property. For a refreshing rustic note, we suggest that you obtain an old wooden wheelbarrow, paint it white and decorate it with elements of folk art, and it will become an appealing flowercart. Fill the interior with flower-

**DECORATIVE BUCKETS**
Old wooden tubs are converted into decorative buckets with many uses just by adding rope handles and designs.

pots. On the side you may want to paint the family name or the street address.

### Picture Frame Becomes Headboard

One young lady we know has devised a novel use for big, old-fashioned picture frames. You may want to carry out her idea if you have a period room. She uses one heavily ornamented frame, with upholstered back, to make an unusual headboard. Of course she has painted it to harmonize with the color scheme of the room.

### A Decorated Bulletin Board

In any kitchen, a small bulletin board of regular builder's wall board, in a picture frame or homemade wooden frame has become a useful part of the homemaker's equipment. Similar bulletin boards, properly brightened with animal figures on a broad frame, can provide a flexible decoration for a nursery—with pictures clipped from magazines and changed regularly. A young college student we know finds such a bulletin board helpful for tacking up notes which require study. Pastel colors and geometric patterns serve to lighten the effect.

### Nail Kegs Into Furniture

Empty nail kegs of varying shapes and sizes, available from your local hardware store, are easily transformed into usable, interesting pieces. They can serve you as scrap baskets, stools, containers for kindling wood, and clothes hampers. The proper color and styling treatment will make them unique. One touch which will help change the personality of a nail keg is a festoon of rope—apply this around the top of the keg. Designs, over a suitable overall color treatment, may be chosen from New England ship or maritime scenes, or from Pennsylvania Dutch, Swedish or Indian motifs.

## HOW TO DECORATE WITH PAINT

To do a successful job of decorating your furniture you will need certain equipment, which includes:

A supply of old newspapers and rags; patching plaster; soap and water; No. 1/2 or No. 1/0 sandpaper; a screwdriver; oxalic acid crystals (or other commercial paint-and-varnish remover if you are working with golden oak pieces); shellac and a 1-inch shellac brush; turpentine (or benzine); tracing paper; Scotch or masking tape; 3H and 2B pencils; ¾-inch and ⅜-inch pointed red sable or good camel hair brushes for oil paints; 1-inch and 4-inch bristle brushes for flat areas (if you are not working with large-surface furniture pieces, substitute a 2-inch brush for the larger size); undercoater or primer paint; flat paint; enamel; tube oil

### CHEST IN SWEDISH STYLE

A richly decorated heart, with angels as cupids, forms the center of this modern combination of folk design elements. Men and maids, tulips nodding in different directions, and a wavy border give the entire piece the gay feeling of springtime. Use Swedish colors recommended in Chapter 3.

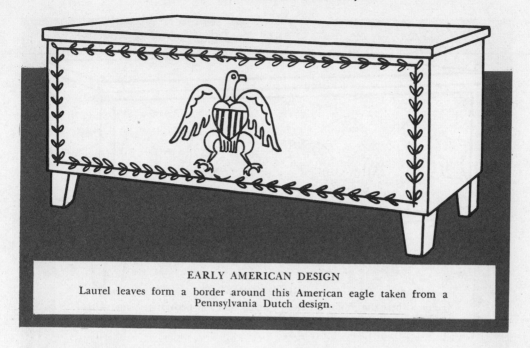

**EARLY AMERICAN DESIGN**
Laurel leaves form a border around this American eagle taken from a
Pennsylvania Dutch design.

paints; linseed oil and an oil cup; a palette (an old plate will do); alcohol for cleaning the shellac brush.

To wash off the acid, use a mixture of one part ammonia and ten parts water. The oxalic acid is also excellent for bleaching wood.

**Sandpapering the Furniture**

First sandpaper the furniture to remove the film of dirt and grease which is there (whether you can see it or not). This gives a better gripping surface for your paint application to adhere to, and prevents blistering or cracking; it is necessary to do this on new unpainted pieces, as well as on old varnished items; an in cases where the wood surface is heavily varnished it is preferable to remove all the varnish or finish, to insure firm application.

**Furniture with Old Finishes**

In working with a piece in which the old finish is in good condition, a light sandpapering with No. 2/0 or No. 3/0 sandpaper may suffice. Before sandpapering, clean the piece, using a cloth saturated in turpentine. This will remove oil, grease and furniture polish; if the piece has been waxed, the process must be repeated several times to insure removal of all the wax. After the cleaning, wipe it dry with a clean cloth. Then apply the sandpaper, and dust off.

If you have done this carefully, and not misjudged the good condition of the previous coat of finish, you will not find it necessary to apply undercoater. Apply one or two coats of enamel finish — if similar in color to the previous treatment, one coat suffices; if you are changing from dark background to

131

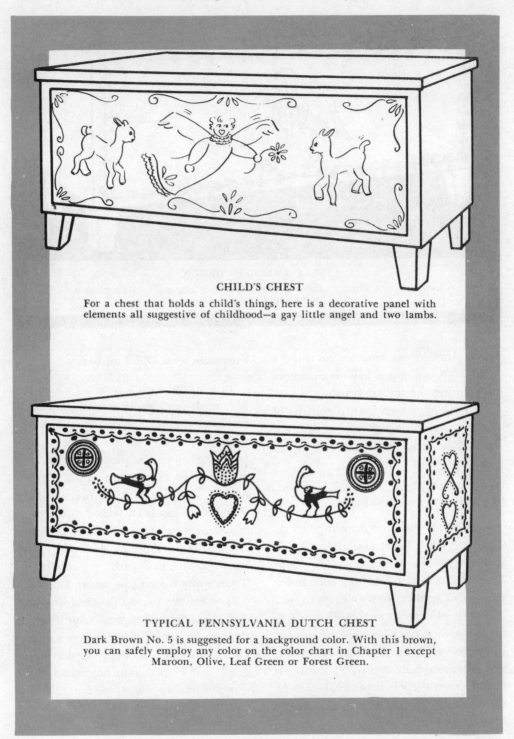

**CHILD'S CHEST**

For a chest that holds a child's things, here is a decorative panel with elements all suggestive of childhood—a gay little angel and two lambs.

**TYPICAL PENNSYLVANIA DUTCH CHEST**

Dark Brown No. 5 is suggested for a background color. With this brown, you can safely employ any color on the color chart in Chapter 1 except Maroon, Olive, Leaf Green or Forest Green.

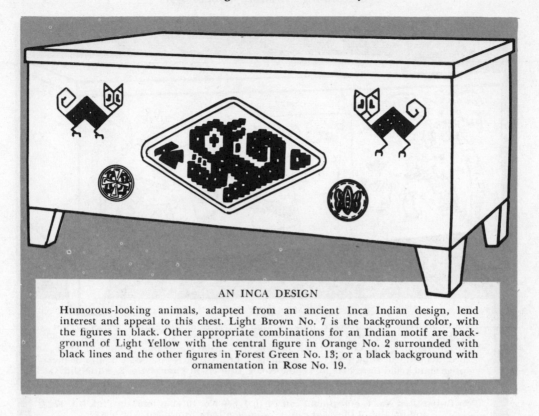

**AN INCA DESIGN**

Humorous-looking animals, adapted from an ancient Inca Indian design, lend interest and appeal to this chest. Light Brown No. 7 is the background color, with the figures in black. Other appropriate combinations for an Indian motif are background of Light Yellow with the central figure in Orange No. 2 surrounded with black lines and the other figures in Forest Green No. 13; or a black background with ornamentation in Rose No. 19.

light, or vice versa, cover with two coats.

If the finish on your old piece of furniture is not in good condition, it is best to use a commercial paint and varnish remover, available at your local hardware, paint or art supply store. If you are working with an old and heavily varnished piece, it may be necessary to use a stiff scraper knife (such as the type used in removing wallpaper) with a three- or four-inch blade. Your remover is available in cream or liquid form; the cream is more suitable for use on vertical surfaces, like the side of a chest, where it will not run down to the floor as readily as liquid will. The liquid varnish or paint remover is more suited

to flat surfaces, such as table tops.

After you have cleared the surface of the old cracking or scaling finish, clean it well with turpentine or benzine. It is particularly important that you do this carefully if the type of varnish or paint remover you purchase has a wax ingredient. The label will tell you if wax is part of the product.

**Quick Way to Remove Old Finish**

Here's another way of getting rid of an old coat of varnish or paint, and bleaching old furniture which you plan to paint and decorate:

Make a saturated solution of oxalic

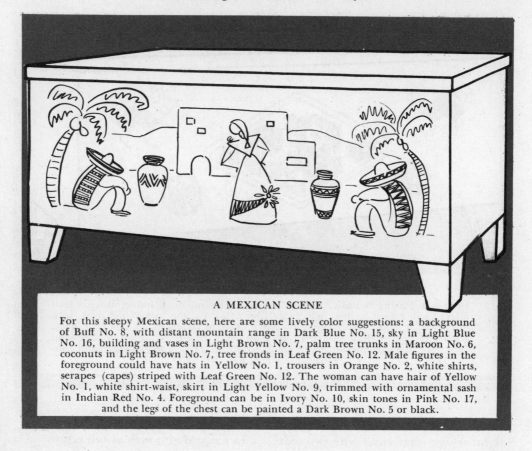

**A MEXICAN SCENE**

For this sleepy Mexican scene, here are some lively color suggestions: a background of Buff No. 8, with distant mountain range in Dark Blue No. 15, sky in Light Blue No. 16, building and vases in Light Brown No. 7, palm tree trunks in Maroon No. 6, coconuts in Light Brown No. 7, tree fronds in Leaf Green No. 12. Male figures in the foreground could have hats in Yellow No. 1, trousers in Orange No. 2, white shirts, serapes (capes) striped with Leaf Green No. 12. The woman can have hair of Yellow No. 1, white shirt-waist, skirt in Light Yellow No. 9, trimmed with ornamental sash in Indian Red No. 4. Foreground can be in Ivory No. 10, skin tones in Pink No. 17, and the legs of the chest can be painted a Dark Brown No. 5 or black.

acid crystals and warm water in a one-quart bottle. This will produce a very strong solution. Pour one-half of this solution into another quart bottle and fill to the top with warm water. These solutions can be stored in a covered jar for future use. Wear rubber gloves when applying all paint and varnish removers.

Tie a soft rag to a stick, and dip the rag into the mixture, then swish it over the furniture from which paint or varnish is to be removed. Wood shavings or sawdust sprinkled over varnish removers will absorb the excess remover and will aid in the easy removal of the sticky residue. Let the furniture stand a few minutes until the old finish softens, then wash it off with hot soapsuds—still wearing the rubber gloves! Wash off the soapsuds and dry the furniture immediately with a cloth.

This process is not to be recommended for furniture of value, but it is a speedy process for preparing old pieces of lesser concern.

**Applying the Primer**

After you have cleaned the piece, it is necessary to "prime" the wood with

## CHILD'S TABLE AND CHAIRS

Since these three pieces really form one group, they are appropriately decorated with related designs. The country scene on the table surface includes a small rooster, which appears enlarged on the seats of the chairs. Designs on the legs are identical. Fill in your own decorations on table and chairs in this way.

**DECORATE YOUR COFFEE TABLE**

The coffee table too gains in charm when you decorate it. A central unit of a heart and flowers — the popular Pennsylvania Dutch theme displayed on several other pieces in this chapter—is bordered with a lengthened version of itself.

a sealing coat of finish—that is, a finish to fill in the pores of the wood; this also covers small scratches or blemishes in the wood surface, and dries quickly so that dust will not collect to mar the appearance of the wood surface. You have a choice of selecting an "undercoater"—which you purchase at your hardware or paint supply store—or of using the "flat" undercoat paint with a touch of enamel paint color added, to give you a darker background.

(A few words of definition may be helpful at this point. A "flat" finish is one that is lusterless, without glossy effect. Your basic coat should be "flat" to make it easier to apply the decorative design. "Enamel" finish is actually a varnish with color added; it is glossy, and does not show brush marks if applied carefully, but will not serve you well as a basic coat for a piece that is to be decorated. Do not overbrush once the paint has set. Enamel finishes can be used successfully where you expect to cover a wooden surface with solid color,

and with no decorative design.)

It is advisable to fill in knotholes with plastic wood or other wood fillers before you apply the undercoat. Brush over these parts with shellac. If new wood is being used, brush over the entire surface with shellac. This will help to fill in the thirsty grain of the wood. Sand lightly before applying the undercoat color.

A valuable point to remember: Cover the floor with newspapers before starting to paint.

In using a large brush for large-surface pieces, be sure that you do not find it necessary to force the brush into the paint can. If the can is too small, pour the paint into a larger container while working, as the brush is ruined for good work when the hairs are disturbed. Apply your brush with light, even strokes. Make strokes horizontally from left to right and then from right to left.

After applying the primer, wash the brushes in turpentine and then in soap and lukewarm water. Between uses,

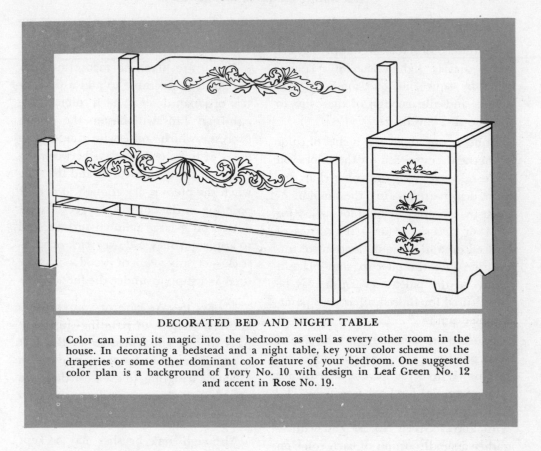

**DECORATED BED AND NIGHT TABLE**

Color can bring its magic into the bedroom as well as every other room in the house. In decorating a bedstead and a night table, key your color scheme to the draperies or some other dominant color feature of your bedroom. One suggested color plan is a background of Ivory No. 10 with design in Leaf Green No. 12 and accent in Rose No. 19.

wipe the brushes clean, wrap them in wax paper (newspaper will do) and lay them flat.

## The Second Coat

In applying your second coat, keep this rule in mind: Use flat paint for the background, tube oil paints for the design. It is hard to draw designs on a glossy surface. So use a matte (or eggshell) type paint surface and apply your design with either a flat or enamel finish.

## How to Trace the Design

Trace the design with a soft (2B) pencil. Then turn your design face down on the furniture on the area you want to decorate; fix it in place with Scotch or masking tape, and retrace the design on the reverse side with a hard (3H) pencil. The outline will come off on the furniture. If you do not wish to have your design come out in reverse, it will be necessary to trace the design on both sides with the soft pencil, and then to go over it with the hard pencil so that the design comes out as you wish it.

## Applying Your Colors

If the colors you are applying are tints—that is, light values of a color—start by squeezing out some of your white, and add enough of the color to get the tint you desire.

Squeeze out about 1½ inches of color from the tubes needed for the colors you have selected from the color chart for your design (regulating the amount of each by the amount of color called for in your design). Pour a few drops of linseed oil and an equal amount of turpentine into the oil cup, and place it handy to the palette. (Varnish may be substituted for linseed oil as your painting medium.)

Squeeze the paints around the side of your palette, leaving the center free for mixing. Where you have a mixed color —for example, for Leaf Green No. 12, which contains Yellow No. 1 together with Forest Green No. 13 and white— gather a small portion of each color on your palette knife and place them in the center of the palette. Mix the colors with your palette knife, adding them to the white.

If your paints do not come out of the tube in the consistency of a paste, dip your brush in the mixture of linseed oil and turpentine, and mix with the paints till the right consistency is obtained. Then, using the sable brushes, except where large areas of solid color permit using a smaller bristle brush, apply your colors to your design.

Apply one color at a time, wiping your brush carefully and cleaning with turpentine, soap and water before going to the next color.

If you are planning to outline your design, it is desirable to add a drop or two of japan dryer to each color before painting. This will hasten the drying process, which otherwise imposes a delay of three or four days between the time you apply your colors and the time when the piece is dry enough to permit painting in the outline. To get at small details on a large painted surface, and to apply outlines, a dowel stick or yardstick — or any strip of wood — may be used as a support under the forearm.

It pays to take care of your brushes between sessions of painting—just as it pays to buy good brushes in the first place. (The cheap brushes always seem to have a dangling, uneven bristle at the side, which is sure to leave its own private brush mark!)

Although some brushes may be kept in jars of turpentine between sessions of painting, it is not possible to stand a sable brush hair-down in a jar—the soft hairs will be bent out of shape. It is necessary to suspend the brushes with string or wire so the hairs do not bear any pressure.

Your unused paints may be left on the palette, and the whole submerged in a dish of water between sessions. The paint will not harden or oxidize under water, and comes out ready for use. The palette should be cleaned with linseed oil when all paints on it have been used up.

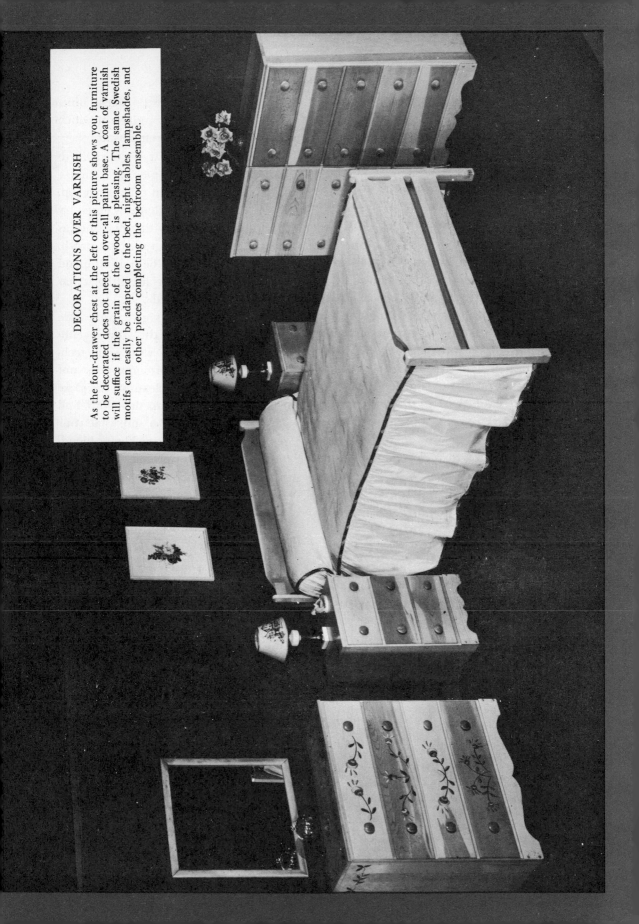

## DECORATIONS OVER VARNISH

As the four-drawer chest at the left of this picture shows you, furniture to be decorated does not need an over-all paint base. A coat of varnish will suffice if the grain of the wood is pleasing. The same Swedish motifs can easily be adapted to the bed, night tables, lampshades, and other pieces completing the bedroom ensemble.

## FINISHING YOUR PIECE

In many cases, you will want the added protection provided by a coat of clear varnish over the painted surface.

This provides an added glossiness to your finish. For outdoor pieces, it provides protection against moisture and weathering.

Another process that has widespread appeal is glazing, by mixing raw Turkey umber with turpentine (three parts) and clear varnish (one part) and linseed oil (a drop). This mixture—which may be varied as to thickness and darkness—is applied with a large brush over the entire surface of the finished piece and quickly rubbed off, so that only a trace of the dark coloring is preserved. A coat of clear varnish may be then applied over the glaze, for a glossy and weather-protected finish.

This glazing process is sometimes referred to as "antiquing" furniture. It gives a mellow effect that makes pieces appear aged, with the rich patina of lengthy service. There need be no implication of fakery or fraud in glazing furniture this way; you are merely seeking to achieve beauty.

First, be sure that the decorated piece is thoroughly dry, before applying your glaze. Then determine whether your decorated piece should have a light or a dark glaze effect. The more of the oil color (the raw Turkey umber) you mix with your turpentine and varnish, the darker your glaze effect will be. To obtain a redder glaze effect, a raw Sienna oil color can be substituted for the umber; an item of furniture decorated in predominantly dark blue, green or red will take a glaze in which lamp black oil color is employed.

For a large object, it is desirable to glaze one part of the piece at a time—drawer by drawer, then sides, then top. The reason for this is that it is necessary to wipe off the glaze with a dry cloth as soon as it has been applied by brush. A dry brush may also be used to blend the glaze on your surface after it has been applied and dried.

The glazing process gives you wide scope for using originality and ingenuity in experimenting with your technique. If the first attempt does not satisfy you, you may clean off the glaze with a turpentine-dampened cloth, and start over again. To be sure that your glaze does not dry too quickly for blending, when you are working with a large surface area, add equal parts of linseed oil to the mixture of varnish and oil paint (the latter mixture, incidentally, is available in ready-mixed form).

The thinner (mineral spirits are better than turpentine because they are slow-drying) should be in the proportion of one part to five.

## DECOUPAGE

Another form of applying decorative ornamentation to furniture is *decoupage*—the mounting of paste-on illustrations skillfully put together into a well laid-out design arrangement, and lacquered over for protection and permanency.

This art, widely practiced in many European countries, was a tremendously

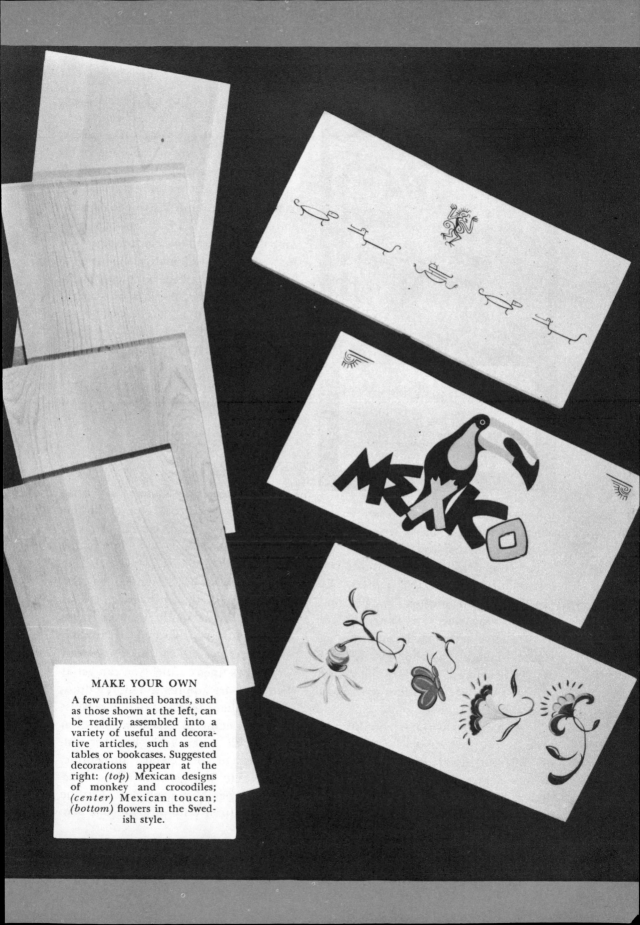

## MAKE YOUR OWN

A few unfinished boards, such as those shown at the left, can be readily assembled into a variety of useful and decorative articles, such as end tables or bookcases. Suggested decorations appear at the right: *(top)* Mexican designs of monkey and crocodiles; *(center)* Mexican toucan; *(bottom)* flowers in the Swedish style.

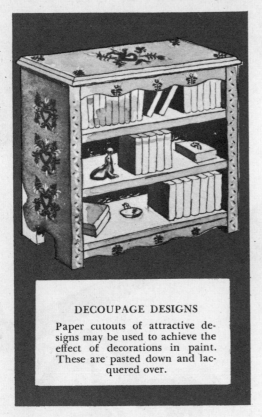

**DECOUPAGE DESIGNS**

Paper cutouts of attractive designs may be used to achieve the effect of decorations in paint. These are pasted down and lacquered over.

cially, should find full range here. Your choice of subject may range from sporting themes to realistic time-pieces placed overly close to the edge of a bureau top, to alarm visitors if carried out with sufficient realism.

It is no more possible to describe all the new materials which you may use, and the new and old techniques you may apply with originality, than it is to catalogue in full all the hobbies and the interests of readers of this book. American inventive genius adds new materials to work with every day. And your own inventive ability and imagination provide the best assurance that you will find a means of restyling your surroundings to suit your personality.

## METALLIC STENCILS ON WOOD

Bronze stenciling is used for decoration on the Hitchcock type of Boston rockers, chairs, trays, boxes, etc. It is usually applied on a flat black paint background, although it may also be used—somewhat less effectively—on deep colors such as red, brown, green, etc. In our opinion, it would be even more effective on a natural wood background.

To make the stencil, use tracing cloth (architect's linen), which you can get at your local art supplier's. This is a durable and pliant material, but care must be taken never to get it wet or even damp with water. It is, however, impervious to oil paint, turpentine, bronzes, etc. Use pen and ink for tracing the design on tracing cloth. Cut the stencil pattern with straight-edge scis-

popular fad during Victorian times, when all sorts of objects were covered with paste-ons and decals.

For your decoupage decorations, collect pictures you like, that express your personality and interests; you can find them in magazine advertisements and illustrations, or in seed catalogues (a source of highly polished examples of artistic printing of flowers), on greeting cards — there are countless sources of appealing design motifs.

The challenge to your originality and taste lies in the combination you make of different floral and other design themes—in your ability to join various design figures into a balanced overall design. Your feeling for color, espe-

sors. For clean, sharp edges, start cutting from the center of an area.

Allow the background paint or varnish to dry thoroughly — at least for twenty-four hours. Then apply a thin coat of twenty-four-hour varnish. When this is no longer sticky, but not yet quite dry, lay the stencil carefully over the area which you wish to decorate. It is best to have the piece of furniture in a horizontal position so that the bronze powder will not slide down between the stencil and the wood surface.

To apply the bronze powder, wrap a piece of silk-backed velvet around the index finger, then dip it in the powder sparingly and dab on the stenciling surface with a horizontal polishing motion. Take up more powder from time to time and apply as though polishing silver. Apply lightly but as often as necessary to get the depth of metal desired.

If you wish to achieve shading, apply the powder more lightly in the dark areas, and as heavily as possible in the highlighted areas. All the powder should be rubbed in firmly so that no loose grains are left before the stencil is picked up. A little experimenting will soon show you how to achieve many interesting effects of shading and highlighting.

It is important to clean the stencil thoroughly on both sides with turpentine before it is used a second time. This is especially true when the stencil is to be reversed. Rub the stencil dry on both sides before applying to a new part of the design. Any tear in the stencil can be mended with Scotch tape.

An interesting effect can be obtained by highlighting the edge of leaves, leaving the center fairly dark, and then applying a second stencil in brilliant highlight showing the veins of the leaves in the center.

Another variation is obtained by making the metallic color fairly uniform and bright and then applying a shaded overlay of oil colors in any desired hue, using the same stencil. Shaded overlays may be achieved with transparent oil colors only. These are yellow lake, Prussian blue, alizarin crimson and raw umber. In general, the overlay is more effective if the color is intense at one side of the stencil and allowed to fade out completely toward the other side. A delicately colored garland of leaves or fruits of various shades can be obtained by this process.

## CHAPTER 6

# Adventures in
# DECORATING TINWARE

In recent years, more and more people have been rediscovering the beauty which can be realized by decorating tinware themselves. Instead of ready-made canisters, boxes, bread and fruit trays or other objects, today we think in terms of converting odd things of tin into practical service or ornaments for the home.

Remember the old tin scoop used for flour barrels? How well this smooth metal takes color! How well its shape is adapted to a wall hanging, lending a touch of color and a bright note of design to the room! The decoration may, for example, carry out the floral design which dominates the slip-cover on the easy chair below. Or, with the help of a handy husband, the necessary wiring attachment and socket may turn the scoop into a wall-lamp, concealing the globe, to reflect the light from the soft wallpaper or plaster tints.

Many a homemaker today spurns the unoriginal, mass-produced canister sets sold in the variety stores. Why not? Vacuum-packed coffee cans, and tin containers in which other staples for the kitchen are sold, provide the raw material for a canister set of varied size. With taste and imagination, the right note of brightness harmonizes with the kitchen curtains, the linoleum, or with figurines painted on the kitchen cabinets.

Or a good-sized dust pan, through quaint design and appealing color, can be converted into an attractive and novel sandwich serving tray.

If you have difficulty obtaining a suitable piece of old tin, the hardware store can supply new tin for your use. But great satisfaction lies in the conversion of old pieces: measuring cups as decorative receptacles to hold flowers; covered tin candy boxes for coffee, tea, sugar, etc.; a scalloped pie pan for purely ornamental use. It's up to you to plan your own original adaptations!

In selecting old pieces to use for decorating—coffee pots, tea pots, syrup jugs, spice boxes, creamers, oil tankards, tin cans, etc.—look for products with good basic design lines. Well-made spouts, hinges, handles and knobs and expert soldering that renders the joints well-nigh invisible, are to be desired if you are buying up old pieces to decorate. The oldtime tinsmith was a master craftsman whose wares are fitting background for your decorative touch!

The country tinware which made its way into early nineteenth-century homes by oxcart and knapsack, more often than not charmed the beholder with decorative designs reflecting nature —fruit, flowers, berries, leaves, sunburst. Backgrounds of black or asphaltum set off the decoration in red, green and yellow, brush-stroked, with borders of white or yellow striping.

## DECORATED CANDLE HOLDER

The candle holder illustrated can be bought ready made, or you can make it from a tin flour scoop, first removing the handle. It will reflect light better if it is left in its original metal color. Flower designs can be applied as shown. Rich Orange No. 2, Leaf Green No. 12, and black stand out effectively against a bright metal background.

## TIN CANISTER SET

Featuring an apple and a pear in a Pennsylvania Dutch treatment. The color plan for the apple could be: Dark Blue No. 15 background, Light Yellow No. 9 for the apple, and the leaves in Leaf Green No. 12. For the smaller unit, the base color could be Indian Red No. 4, with the pear colored in Buff No. 8 and the leaves in Leaf Green No. 12.

## MATERIALS NEEDED

What materials do we need for our adventure in tin?

*For Brushwork.* Square-tipped, fine ¾-inch French quill brushes 1/16 and ⅛ inches wide (if the volume of work you plan is limited, you may desire to compromise on using a 3/32-inch brush only); fine-pointed quills, or sable water-color brushes, in these same sizes, may be substituted. Also needed are showcard brushes, ¼ and ⅜ inch wide; quality varnish brushes for applying flat paint or varnish; a 1½-inch striping brush; India ink; crow quill pen.

*For Paints.* Add japan drier to the oil paints recommended in our chapter on color. Or, if you are not planning any work other than in tin, get your colors ground in japan (that is, in japan base). Also, quality flat paint; turpentine for washing brushes, and carbon tetrachloride for erasing mistakes (also for removing rust-remover).

(Japan is both a drying agent, which can be added to regular oil paints to give them a quick-drying quality, and a color medium in which you may buy paints. Japan is available at the average

**DECORATE A COFFEE POT**

Your old-fashioned coffee pot may have been replaced by more modern devices, but it can still serve as a handsome ornament if you will decorate it like this one, with a Swedish tulip.

**QUAINT WATERING CAN**

The quaint shape of an old watering can gains in charm when you add designs such as these, which are simple variations of the fruits appearing in Chapter 2.

hardware or paint store, and at many art supply stores. Colors in japan—or to which japan has been added—will come out in a glossy, hard finish; it is therefore unnecessary to varnish over the piece after you have applied your decorations in japan colors, unless the piece is subject to hard use. In any event, one coat of japan should be sufficient on tin. The quick-drying quality lessens the danger that dust will accumulate on the decorated object while it is still wet or tacky.)

*For Preparing the Metal.* Rust-remover; a common cleansing compound, preferably of trisodium type, which includes most popular brands; metal priming paint, carbon tetrachloride.

*For Finishing.* The finest wet-or-dry garnet sandpaper; fine pumice; rottenstone (very fine); crude or mineral oil.

*For Recording and Tracing Designs.* Tracing paper; a yard of transparent acetate-plastic sheets (sketching is done on the dull surface); Scotch tape; drawing pencil No. 1H; blackboard chalk or magnesium carbonate, obtainable at drug stores.

*For Stenciling.* Architect's linen; embroidery scissors; razor blade; chamois

**COVERED TIN CONTAINER**

Fruit and leaves, drawn by the methods described in Chapter 2, combine well in an over-all design for a covered tin container. Other chapters show you many more designs you can use to decorate your tinware.

**FOR YOUR LETTERS**

Showing a tin stationery holder for desk use. A suggested color treatment, if you do not wish to use the natural tin color for a background, would include a base color of Pink No. 17, Maroon No. 6 for lettering or initials, Leaf Green No. 12 and white for other design features.

**LIGHT BACKGROUND SETS OFF DESIGN**

Showing a tissue dispenser and a waste basket decorated with large-figure graceful floral patterns.
Notice how the light background color makes the design stand out in bold relief.

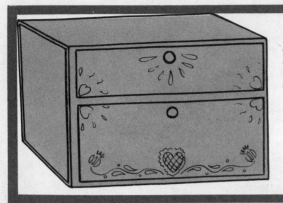

**COLORFUL BREAD BOX**

The bread box goes Pennsylvania Dutch with just a few brush strokes and the right color note. In this instance, a color scheme consisting of Dark Brown No. 5 background with bright Indian Red No. 4, Leaf Green No. 12, and Purple-Blue No. 3 achieves a pleasing effect.

or silk-backed velvet; bronze powders (rich gold, orange gold, pale gold, aluminum); transparent colors (alizarin crimson, Prussian blue, yellow lake, raw umber); gloss varnish.

## PRACTICING YOUR DESIGN

Now we have our equipment lined up. The first step, of course, is the selection of designs. The chapters of this book relating to decorative design have offered a varied selection—but perhaps you want to try your hand, or to record a design before working with the tin.

Place your acetate-plastic sheet over the pattern to be copied, attaching it

with Scotch tape. Paint on this sheet the undercoats—that is, the basic color or colors—of flowers, leaves, and other basic features of the design. Then lift the transparent sheet from the design,

**TRY TULIPS ON YOUR HAMPER**

Illustrating how a tin or fiber laundry hamper may be ornamented with a simple Swedish tulip border design. In this instance, a white background may be combined with a choice among Yellow No. 1, Orange No. 2 or Indian Red No. 4, Purple-Blue No. 3 and Light Green No. 14 to carry the Swedish motif into a typical color treatment.

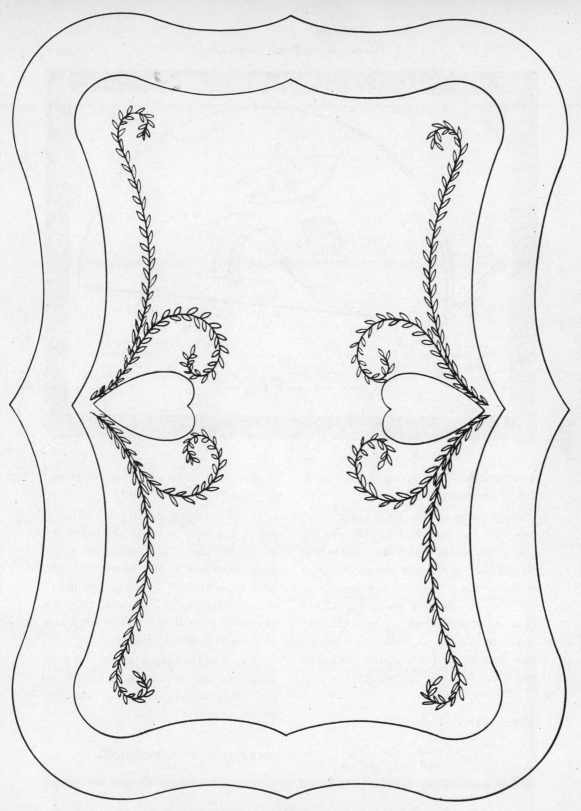

## HEART AND WREATH PATTERN
Showing a delicate Swedish design that should present no problems to the beginner in decorating tinware.

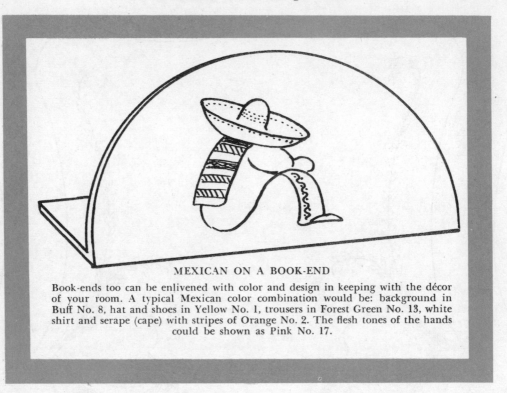

MEXICAN ON A BOOK-END

Book-ends too can be enlivened with color and design in keeping with the décor of your room. A typical Mexican color combination would be: background in Buff No. 8, hat and shoes in Yellow No. 1, trousers in Forest Green No. 13, white shirt and serape (cape) with stripes of Orange No. 2. The flesh tones of the hands could be shown as Pink No. 17.

and attach it to a piece of cardboard. Let it dry overnight.

Now paint on the details, the overtones — the semi-transparent tinting tones that shade your design and give it life. This is good practice—and it may come in handy to have this copy later on. Preserve the thin sheet—it's thicker than cellophane wrapping, but still very light—by taping it with your Scotch tape to a piece of heavy paper and placing it in a wax-paper envelope.

## PREPARING THE TIN

Now to prepare your tin. If your metal is new, sand it lightly. Scrub it in hot, soapy water to remove filmy oil or grease, then rinse in hot water and dry quickly and thoroughly.

If you are using an old piece of metal which has been painted previously, remove all paint with standard paint remover or boil it in a solution of common cleanser—half a box to a gallon of water. Clean it of rust with the rust-remover you will find in any hardware store—and some elbow-grease!

If your old tin requires use of a rust-remover, use carbon tetrachloride to get the solvent off, then scrub with hot, soapy water and wipe dry.

## SANDING AND PRIMING

A light sanding with very fine garnet

PENNSYLVANIA DUTCH ROOSTER

wet-or-dry sandpaper is your next step. Now for your priming coat. Any standard metal priming paint which can be brushed on is suitable, or you might mix a little varnish with flat black paint, or use clear varnish. In any case, you are assured by use of the priming coat that your design will not crack or peel after you have painted your tinware.

As a background, we recommend black paint because it is an effective foil for most colors. If you prefer something other than black, use such oil colors as vermilion, ultramarine, chrome yellow medium, sienna or umber (for golden shades) or veridian (green).

After the priming, apply two or three coats of flat paint, allowing a twenty-four hour drying period for each, and using a little turpentine if thinner is needed. Sand lightly between coats, or rub down with a mosquito netting well crumpled. The advantage of a flat black background will be seen when you come to the painting of your design. In case of error you can always touch it up with your flat black and paint over but be sure you save the flat black you have previously used. It's amazing how many shades of flat black will turn up in different cans with the same label!

## HOW TO TRANSFER YOUR DESIGN

You're ready now to paint. Copy your design on a piece of ordinary tracing paper, using a No. 1H pencil. Cover the back of the tracing lightly with chalk, brushing off excess; then put the tracing on the tinware, attaching it firmly with Scotch tape, and retrace your pattern. The chalk lines on the tin will guide your placement of the design, and the general proportions of your decorative pattern. Of course, when you have had a little practice, you will be ready to skip the tracing process and do your decoration with the mechanical aids already advocated — compass, French curve and ruler. With experience and confidence you will no doubt want to try your hand at working in freehand.

## PAINTING ON TIN

Let's say you're making a wall-lamp of a tin scoop for a rumpus room. Perhaps the fighting cock on page 176 will appeal to you. For color, No. 4 on the color chart appeals to you as a red.

(For a milder, softer red, such as you might want on a coffee tray, the addition of raw umber would do the trick.)

Spread your paints on an old plate, pie-tin, or tin can cover, stirring with a wooden matchstick. Pour some varnish —which is used as your medium with which the paint is applied—into a jar cover; dip the paintbrush into the varnish, and then "pull" it through the paint. It takes practice to determine how much paint to use.

In brush-stroking your paint on the tin, apply the brush down flat (almost parallel to your work surface), for the large end of the stroke, lifting it to bring your stroke end up to a fine point, steadying your hand the while with

### DESIGN FOR A CANISTER

In this balanced design for a tin canister, combining typical Pennsylvania Dutch figures of bird, tulip and heart, note how the birds eyes give life to the whole theme. At lower right, the artist's signature lends a personal touch—when decorating your own, don't hesitate to do the same.

PUT FRUIT ON YOUR TRAY

Ivory No. 10 is suggested as a background color. Leaf Green No. 12, Buff No. 8, Light Brown No. 7, Dark Blue No. 15 and black will serve to accent the design detail.

your little finger. The old-time painting on tin was done thinly—so go easy on the paint. Remember this cardinal rule: *Paint toward yourself,* holding the tinware you are decorating so that this may be done. Try to keep the edge of your brush stroke clean, and run your curves smoothly, without jerking the wrist.

If you want the body of the red rooster opaque, use two coats, twenty-four hours apart. Your overtones—in the Orange No. 2 (see color chart in Chapter 1) — are applied even more thinly. Extra varnish on the brush—and a lighter touch in the paint — give a slight translucency. But be careful not

to get too much varnish on the brush, or your paint will run after the stroke.

Your overtones must be applied after the basic colors have dried completely, if you would avoid the danger of smudging.

### How to Paint Borders

Now let's say you want a border band of white. Country tin pieces of the past used either bands or stripes—mostly not in clear white, but with a grayed, translucent look, obtained by mixing a little raw umber and a speck of yellow ochre to your titanium white.

## Ideas for Decorating Tinware

Whatever the piece of tinware—be it new or old—there is a design that will make it serve its purpose more handsomely. *(Top left)* An old watering can with Norwegian designs and scrolls added can still be as useful, or assume a new role as a vase or purely ornamental piece. *(Top right)* A dipper, a pitcher and two trays made gay with designs, and *(right)* a wastepaper basket with a quaint horse and rider that can reappear on a desk or chest of drawers. *(Bottom row)* Children's lunch boxes with nursery pictures, and a coal hod in the Pennsylvania Dutch style that is now ready to hold magazines.

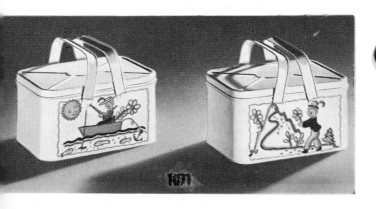

# *Plain Metal Objects Transformed*
## *Into Things of Charm and Beauty*

*(Right)* Toy roasting pan and bread tin with flower decorations.

*(Left)* Heavy old-fashioned flat irons decorated with a foundation coat of white paint and Pennsylvania Dutch designs.

*(Right)* A scoop, a box, and two trays with Swedish, Pennsylvania Dutch, and conventional designs.

THEME FOR COCKTAILS

For a cocktail tray, pink elephants form an appropriate design. The background
might be black or gray. You can trace and enlarge these elephants by the use
of squares, explained in Chapter 2.

Your striping should be applied twenty-four hours after one coat of varnish has been applied to the tinware, as part of the finishing process. In striping, mix your paint and varnish medium—note the difference from the preceding process in painting the design—and then draw the striping brush through the mixture. Try it out on a piece of paper, watching for specks of paint that have not mixed evenly. Your mixture should be of a free-flowing consistency, thin, clear, and smooth. Now hold the striping brush between thumb and forefinger, running third and fourth fingers along the edge to steady the hand. Pull the brush toward you—smoothly and steadily, and not too slowly.

If you're painting a white band, instead of a stripe, it may be best for you to paint two guide lines with striping technique, and then to fill in your band with broad strokes between the guide lines. Your border band is painted on with the same mixture used for the narrower stripe. If you're uncertain in your touch, you may want to use the tracing technique for borders.

Quills are used for decorative painting and for painting in the guide lines for a wide band. A showcard brush is used to fill in the space between the two guide lines.

## HOW TO USE
## STENCIL TECHNIQUE

Maybe you'll prefer to use the stenciling technique to transfer your chosen designs onto tin.

Trace your design onto ordinary tracing paper with India ink and a crow quill pen. Cut a piece of architect's linen at least one inch larger all around than the pattern. Trace your decorative design onto the piece of linen with India ink, and cut the stencil with embroidery scissors and knife. The scissors is good for small curves, and to cut small dots with the point tips. The knife is good for open curves or straight lines; on fine lines, such as flower stems, cut one side of the line with the knife and pare it down to desired width with the scissors.

### Applying the Stencil

Now to apply the stencil. First give tin one smooth, even coat of varnish. (This can be done over a paint finish.) When the varnish is tacky, but not quite dry (if you touch it, the finger comes away dry, but there is a "sticky" touch), you are ready to apply the stencil; this is normally a half-hour's wait, depending on room temperature, amount of varnish used, etc.

Next, place the stencil in correct position on the tinware. Wrap around your forefinger a small piece of chamois or silk-backed velvet (cotton or rayon will not do the job). Hold the stencil in place with your left hand (I'm assuming you're right-handed!) and dip the chamois carefully into the bronze powder you have selected. Don't use too much! Apply the powder to the tacky varnished surface of the tin with a circular motion, shading the design where required by repeating the process in the areas to be shaded, thereby increasing the amount of powder.

After the stenciled tinware has dried for twenty-four hours, wash away loose powder under running water. Touch up with flat black where the powder has gone out of place. And, if you want to save the stencil for further use, clean it with turpentine—not water!

### How to Apply Overtones

Overtones may be applied by laying broad brush strokes of thin transparent color over the different parts of the design. In the old stenciled designs, these overtones were placed on to groups of leaves or petals by applying the transparent color in one stroke, rather than used to define the color for each individual unit.

You use the same technique for striping and finishing stenciled tinware as you do in brush-stroke painting.

## HOW TO FINISH TINWARE

Whether your decorative design is applied by means of tracing, freehand brush-stroking or stenciling, the finish-

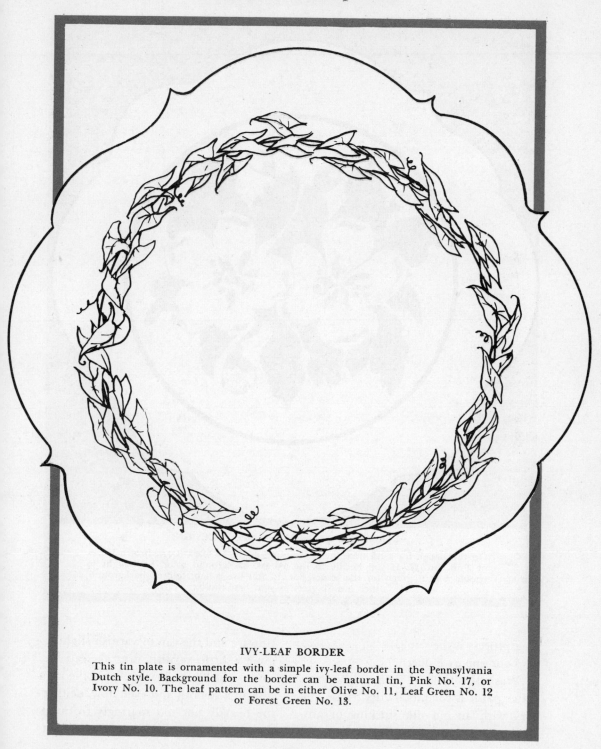

### IVY-LEAF BORDER

This tin plate is ornamented with a simple ivy-leaf border in the Pennsylvania Dutch style. Background for the border can be natural tin, Pink No. 17, or Ivory No. 10. The leaf pattern can be in either Olive No. 11, Leaf Green No. 12 or Forest Green No. 13.

**DOGWOOD BLOSSOMS MAKE A DESIGN**

On this design for a tin tray, the background might be black, Dark Brown No. 5, or Pink No. 17. If you decide to use a dark background color, you ought to choose a light green for the leaves. Should you use a light-colored background, then a dark green is your best choice.

ing process is the same.

Your enemy is dust!

Wash the tinware with soapy water after paint is completely dry, rinse, and dry with an old silk stocking or anything else that is lint-free. Warm the tinware and the can of varnish slightly; pour a little varnish into a clean jar cover, and fill the brush. Apply the varnish in a smooth and even flow, neither too heavily nor too sparingly to cause the varnish to run. Don't stand a flat

### DESIGN IDEA FOR TIN PLATE
The rim and the baby lamb can be left in natural tin color. The rest of the decoration can be in Forest Green No. 13, Dark Blue No. 15, or Rose No. 19. White, Ivory No. 10 or Buff No. 8 can be used as a secondary color if desired.

piece on end while drying—this also can cause the varnish to run. Cover the tinware with a dust-protecting box for twenty-four hours while waiting for it to dry—use a box big enough to provide ventilation.

After the first coat has dried, apply another coat.

*Some Hints and Warnings.* Don't shake the can of varnish before using, or tiny air bubbles will form, ruining your smooth finish and requiring an

### HEX SIGN ON A TRAY
This hex sign lends itself to stencil reproduction in a Pennsylvania Dutch treatment. The central circle and the hearts might be in red, the triangles in yellow.

162

endless wait before they disappear. Never dip your brush directly in the varnish can. Never leave the cover off the can. Pick a dry day—and work in a room with temperature over 70 degrees.

A good grade of satin-finish varnish can be used for smaller objects that do not have to be water- and alcohol-proof, but for trays and other finer tinware items bar-top or spar varnishes are needed. And for an attractive finish, rub down the tinware with a soft, wet cloth dipped in pumice and crude oil, forty-eight hours after application of the second coat. Apply until a smooth finish is obtained, eliminating any dust specks. Then give it a final polishing with rottenstone and crude oil, taking care not to rub through the varnish, especially around the edges.

Now you have an ornamental item of tinware, in which you may take pride.

## CHAPTER 7

# PAINTING TILES and POTTERY

Clay, like tin, offers a wonderful medium for the home decorator's art. You can buy unpainted pieces—jugs, vases, dishes, or other things—at very little cost and turn them into objects that are attractive as well as useful. You can engage in a fascinating new hobby—decorating your own tiles—and use them in the many ways that we shall suggest.

To preserve your designs on clay, you will need to fire them. Sometimes you can do this in your kitchen oven, but in certain cases you will require a kiln. The expense is small in comparison to the beauty tiles add to your home.

Let's see, first of all, what you can do with tile.

## TILE IN OUR HOMES

As ever, we Americans want to make our homes fit the personality of the people who live in them. The use of tile is one more field for self-expression. Not only can you pick out the color you want, but you can with little difficulty paint your own choice of a color scheme and decorative design on your tile surfaces.

Tile surfaces offer many advantages. For one thing, tile is waterproof. It is easy to clean, grease-proof and acid-proof; it is sanitary and durable. Changes in temperature do not affect it —so tile with your designs can be used on the walls behind a stove or in other places exposed to heat.

Most important of all, tile is colorfast. Once your design has been baked into the clay tile, it never needs varnishing, painting, or other retouching. There is no redecorating to worry about, because your tile is permanent. You do have this problem to face: your color and decorative designs must be chosen carefully, because you're going to have to live with them for a long,

long time! But that means saving money—and so it's worth the careful thought you give to planning your tile.

The best inspiration for the modern decorator of tile lies in some of the original uses that have been thought up for it.

Sinclair Lewis, the famous author, has a tile-topped table for chess and checkers, the squares laid out in checkerboard pattern in two colors.

I know of one household in which the daughter of the house was given an attractive headboard for her bed, made by tile-surfacing an unpainted bookcase on top, sides, and back.

A tile shield over the bathroom radiator may be built to add a handy and attractive towel shelf.

A window sill, surfaced with ceramic tiles, makes an ideal spot for an indoor garden. The tiles are moisture-proof, and the "sweating" of flowerpots does not damage them; those that are not covered by the flowerpots may be charmingly decorated.

For families with young children, an attractive and practical novelty is a

**TILED WINDOW SILL**

A tiled window sill provides an attractive and useful surface for an indoor garden. It is easier to clean and does not blister when water seeps through the base of an over-filled flowerpot occasionally. An added note of interest can be achieved by coloring the pots.

Try tiles on a vanity table or a small bookcase. The piece will look twice as handsome if several of the tiles bear your decorations. The designs suggested—a grouping of flowers, a house and tree made of basic curves and straight lines, a tulip painted in two colors—can be easily duplicated, or you can create your own designs for the purpose.

youth-sized table paved with ceramic tiles, for play and for dining. Such a table may be made with little difficulty. Get from a lumber yard several good boards of seasoned wood, and make a table three feet square, with legs two and a half feet in height; or purchase a table in the unpainted furniture department of a local store, and if necessary, cut down the legs to proper height. The top may be surfaced with three dozen unglazed ceramic tiles, each 4½ inches by 4½ inches. Suitable decoration of the tile may be made by following the instructions in this chapter.

One father, with twin sons, designed a table with an alphabet facing either way, so that the two boys could play on opposite sides of the table and learn the letters.

A table of this sort, for small fry, is a blessing to mother, too. At mealtime, a tile-surfaced table offers little concern over spilled foods.

Coffee tables, too, gain in charm and sparkle when you top them with tile. Tiles may be used to frame fireplaces, for wall areas or drainboards, or they may be hung on the wall as ornaments. There is no limit to the places and ways you can use them effectively in home decoration.

## APPLYING TILE SURFACES

In making a tile-topped table, the first step after you have the table and tile is to waterproof the top surface with a standard wood sealer or a couple of coats of varnish. Whether you are doing

## ALPHABET ON A TILE

You can paint the entire alphabet on a single tile and use it as a decorative plaque for the child's room or as a "coaster" for his milk and cookies.

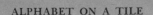

aBCDeFG
HIJKLMN
OPQRSTU
VWXYZ·&
1234567890

TILES ON OUR TEA WAGON

The top of a tea wagon provides the tile decorator with an opportunity to apply his art in a practical manner.

# HOW TO SURFACE A

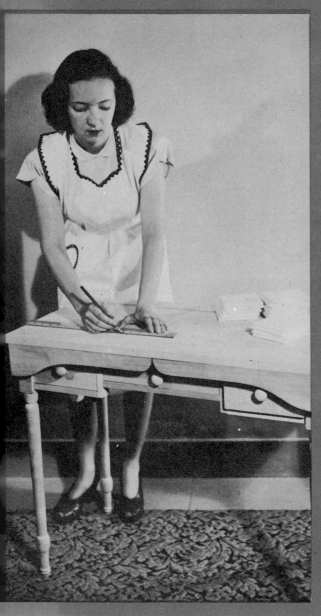

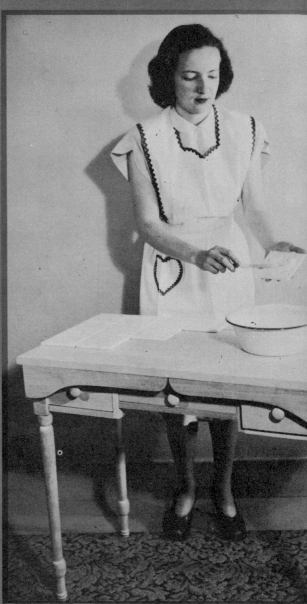

1. On the table surface, rule in pencil the position of all tiles as a guide for laying them on in proper position.

2. "Butter" the tiles with an adhesive cement as each is ready for placement on the table. The lengthwise row along one edge of the table should be set into position first as a guide for the other rows.

# TABLE WITH TILES

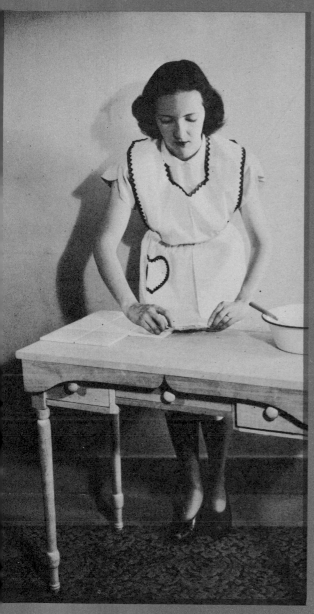

3. Hold tile by the edges and place it in position as shown.

4. When tiles are all laid, and have set overnight, fill in the eighth-inch space between tiles with a cement mixture. Of course you should decorate your tiles before placing them on the table.

### TILE FRAME FOR A FIREPLACE

Decorated tiles furnish a handsome frame for a fireplace. Use of two or three different designs lends a pleasing variety to the over-all effect.

### DESIGN ON A COFFEE TABLE

Two good tracings might be used to reproduce this design on your tiles. The color scheme should be bold, and needs no more than one color to prove effective. The table legs should be in the same color as the dominant one used in the design.

your own color and design treatments on your tile, or buying already decorated tile from your local art or department store, you should find no difficulty in laying the tile on the table yourself. The tile is attached to the table by means of an adhesive or "mastic," available at hardware stores or the five-and-ten. Adhesive cement is for sale at stores in every community. The adhesive is applied to the back of each tile which is then set on the table. Allow 1/8 inch between the tiles. Let the tile set overnight, and then fill in the space between tiles with water and portland cement, mixed to the consistency of cream.

If your tile pieces leave an uncovered gap at the edge of your table, you may do one of four things:

1. Buy tile strips for the border, either 1/2 inch or 1 inch in width.

2. Take tiles to a tile contractor's, to be cut to the necessary size to fill out to the edge of the table.

3. Rim the table with quarter-round mouldings obtainable from any lumber dealer.

4. Buy a glass cutter at the dime store, and score the surface of the tile piece to fit your end space—then tap with a hammer gently on the back of the tile, and it will break off cleanly at this point.

With the tile top of the table in place, a coat of paint for the legs and apron of the homemade or unpainted store table completes the job.

While the new adhesives make tile-setting of this type—and even for modest wall or floor installations—a possibility for every homemaker, you may wish to call on the services of your local contractor for tile-setting and confine your efforts to decorating the tile.

## GETTING YOUR TILE

Suitable tile is made from clay and/or other ceramic materials. It comes in a great variety of sizes and shapes, with many different body compositions, colors and finishes.

There are two general types—glazed and unglazed. A glazed tile surface will not absorb stains or change color. Glazed tile has a glass-like finish which may be clear or opaque, white or black, colored or polychrome. It may have a smooth, mottled, veined or rippled effect. A glazed finish may be bright or semi-matte (between bright and eggshell) or matte (eggshell). In choosing the type of glazed finish, you may prefer a soft matte glaze which will diffuse light for wall areas, table tops and drainboards, for borders around a fireplace, etc.

Unglazed tile has no glaze on the surface. The same ingredients are used throughout the tile as appear on its face.

Sizes of tile range from small "dots" 11/32 inches square to 9 inches square, and thicknesses vary from 1/4 inch to 1 1/2 inches.

You may buy tile from dime stores or hardware stores, or from a local tile contractor or tile wholesaler. If you have any difficulty, the Tile Council of America, at 10 East 40th Street in New

York City, makes it a practice to provide you with the names and addresses of dealers nearest your home who will furnish you with finished or unfinished tile. The cost of a 6-inch by 6-inch tile or a 4¼ by 4¼ is very low.

You can, of course, purchase already-decorated tile from art or department stores. But as this book is dedicated to the help of those who wish to "do it themselves," the next step is to consider how to decorate unfinished tile.

## DECORATING YOUR TILES

If you want to decorate your tile on a temporary basis only, you may put your design on with a quick-drying enamel paint; this of course cannot be baked into the tile for permanence. The enamel design will last for several months. At the end of that period, you will have to renew the design or put on a different one. Unbaked designs last on tile only until smeared.

For those who are content to place attractive designs and color arrangements on either tile or pottery, without attempting to make them permanent by firing them into the ceramic material, the use of oil paints—"cold water paint-

---

### DESIGNS FOR YOUR TILES

To reproduce the designs on this and the next three pages, follow the easy methods described in Chapter 2. For the more complicated figures, it is best to trace and enlarge, using squares. These also serve as a guide to placing the parts of the designs correctly.

Against a white background, paint the main body of the peacock Light Green No. 14, with tail Forest Green No. 13 and wings in Light Brown No. 7. Star portions of floral pattern and decorative elements might be **Rose** No. 19. Paint remaining leaves and stems in Light Green No. 14 and with touches of Light Brown No. 7.

In this scene depicting a ship sailing against the wind, the background is white, the water directly under the ship Light Green No. 14, and the clouds are Light Blue No. 16. The ship, the darker half of the sails and the sea are Maroon No. 6. The other half of the sails and half of the flag are Light Yellow No. 9. The darker portion of the flag is Purple-Blue No. 3.

Two tulips, a daisy, and leaves stand out against a background of Light Blue No. 16, edged with white in this design. You may paint the flowers in any appropriate color— we recommend Pink No. 17. Black and Olive No. 11 would be good for accent touches.

Light Green No. 14 for the apple and black-berries, Purple-Blue No. 3 for the grapes, and Light Blue No. 16 for the apple leaves might be your palette for this still-life.

This rooster would look good on a tile plaque. The background is white, and a large portion of the decorative features of the bird, as well as the tree twig on which he stands, may be painted in Light Blue No. 16. The comb and leaf elements and a portion of the tail contrast well in Rose No. 19. Black is the only other color needed.

Dogwood blossoms and buds make up the design on this tile. The background and blossoms are white. Rose No. 19 edges the blossoms. Paint the leaves Forest Green No. 13, and put touches of Blue No. 3 in the calyx, with green.

ing," as the ceramics specialists call it— can produce more beautiful results.

## Materials Needed

When you use tube oil paints on tile or pottery, your equipment should include: Tube oil paints described in Chapter 1; two round sable brushes, in 1/4-inch and 1/16-inch size; a flat sable brush; spar varnish or clear shellac; turpentine; tracing paper, grease ceramic crayon or soft drawing pencil; Scotch tape or masking tape.

If you are working with tile and pottery for the first time, it will be best for you to use a base coat of varnish or shellac. If you do this, it is easier to remove any errors with turpentine.

## How to Transfer Designs

Now to transfer the design of your preference to your tile or pottery wares. First cut a sheet of tracing paper to the size of the decorative design you have chosen. Trace the design on the sheet of thin paper. Reverse the paper, and copy the lines of the design with the crayon or soft drawing pencil. (This enables you to make the single tracing sheet act as a carbon paper. You place the tracing over a sheet of carbon paper, and transfer your sketch onto your tile or pottery ware by using carbon paper in this way; but because of the awkward shape and size of tile, and particularly of pottery and other ceramic pieces, it is better to use the reverse side of your tracing sheet

177

NUMBERS ON TILE

These numbers, suitable for your house front, show Pennsylvania Dutch motifs adapted to easy lettering forms. Background is white, the lettering Forest Green No. 13, the flowers Indian Red No. 4, and scrollwork connecting the flowers is white.

as carbon by retracing the design with crayon or soft drawing pencil.)

After the reverse side of the tracing sheet has been marked, fasten the tracing sheet onto your pottery ware with Scotch or masking tape, taking care to place it in proper position to get the design where you want it. The crayon or soft-pencil side of the sheet should of course face downward.

To transfer the tracing onto your pottery wares, redraw on the original side of the sheet. The crayon or soft-pencil will come off in the design motif outline. The design can also be transferred by penciling over the entire area; this will also cause the crayon or soft-pencil outline to come off onto the tile. The same technique is applicable, of course, whenever you have a problem in transcribing designs onto wood, paper, or other surfaces.

### How to Paint on Burnt Clay

After your tracings are transferred to the various pieces with which you are going to work, mix your colors, providing enough of each of the colors you plan to use in your designs so that it will not be necessary to make more later. Matching can be a difficult problem, and even where you use an unmixed color from a single tube, the beginner is apt to get different thicknesses with successive mixtures.

Use an old plate, glass piece, or clean flat metal for mixing your colors; add a drop or two of varnish, and thin with turpentine until your mixture is of the consistency of heavy cream.

Apply paint to large areas first, avoiding the use of too much paint on the brush. When you plan to use the brush in a different color, clean it thoroughly

### DESIGN FOR A TRAY

Two tulips pointing in different directions make a simple but dramatic design for a tile tray.

### REPEATED DESIGN

Designs repeated just a few times in one decorative unit are not monotonous. This design for a tile tray is adapted from an Indian border. Keep the colors simple—two are enough.

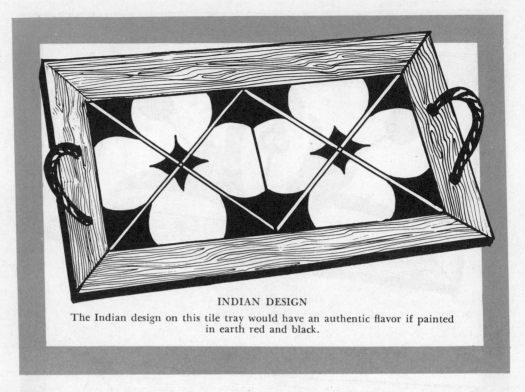

**INDIAN DESIGN**

The Indian design on this tile tray would have an authentic flavor if painted in earth red and black.

in turpentine and wash in soap and water.

The painted design should be given a period of one to two weeks for drying in a place fairly protected from dust. A coat of varnish will protect your design from wearing off or smearing. But if the piece is to undergo handling or contact with other objects, it will require more permanent decoration.

## PERMANENT CERAMICS DECORATION

Permanent decoration of pottery—either tile or ornamental pottery wares—involves the use of ceramic paints, and the baking of your design and colors into the clay tile after it has been applied.

### Materials Needed

You need the following equipment: Ceramic paint, in powder or in solid form; a greasy lead pencil; a fine paintbrush ($\frac{1}{8}$ inch); a medium-size paintbrush ($\frac{1}{4}$ inch); sevco gum; turpentine; fat oil; glass slab; spatula for mixing.

It probably will not be a part of your plans to go so deeply into tile or pottery decoration that you will want to get your own firing kiln. However, it is of interest that you can purchase a simple kiln, which plugs into your electric outlet, for between thirty and forty dollars.

**TRY THIS ON A DISH**

Showing a pleasing design of a bird and tulips in a Pennsylvania Dutch treatment.
Three borders are used: an outer band, a continuous flower-and-leaf pattern,
and a scrollwork figure.

You must select your tile before buying your coloring materials, as there are different materials used for glazed and for unglazed tile. These are *not* interchangeable. Glazed tiles are easier for beginners to work with. Your local paint store should be able to direct you to the nearest ceramics supply store for the special paints; many leading department stores now carry them; and you will find any art supply or hobby-craft shop helpful.

**Working With Solid Paints**

The beginner who desires to work

**IN THE NORWEGIAN STYLE**

An arresting, modern decorative note is created by these easily applied lines for a Norwegian after-dinner coffee service. A suitable color combination could be Forest Green No. 13, Purple-Blue No. 3, Indian Red No. 4, or Maroon No. 6 on a background of Ivory No. 10 or white.

with a coloring medium which can give his pottery or tile the permanence imparted by firing can obtain from art stores or hobby-craft shops a simple set of solid ceramic decorating colors, which in appearance resemble the colors in a water-color set. These are semi-moist, water-soluble, and ready for immediate use on glazed or unglazed clay (ceramics) or china ware. Be sure to obtain the set appropriate for your pottery or china—overglaze colors for glazed pieces, and underglaze colors for unglazed pieces.

Although you have less range of color variety in these sets than you do in the use of powders, it is possible to intermix these non-flowing colors to obtain a close approximation of the colors you choose from the Color Chart in Chapter 1.

The same supply stores have available sets of color for ceramics decoration in liquid form. And a plastic liquid glaze available for pottery or glassware gives you a choice of a variety of effects.

After cleaning the surface with a glaze reducer that comes with the set, you paint onto the surface a white glaze base coat. Then for a transparent-color effect, apply two thin coats of the glaze, using a quick stroke; allow twenty minutes' drying time after the base coat, and between coats. An opaque effect is

**NORWEGIAN PLATES AND PITCHER**

Although they are simple, these decorations are nonetheless effective, and success-fully adapted to the areas which they occupy. With a background of Ivory No. 10, suggested accent colors are Yellow No. 1, Orange No. 2, Purple-Blue No. 3, and Light Green No. 14.

obtainable by adding more coats of the same color; a high-luster finish by adding several coats of clear transparent glaze over the entire decorated surface. This set offers a glaze reducer for correcting errors, for thinning the colors, and for cleaning the brushes.

A metallic effect can be obtained by adding gold, silver or bronze powders to the transparent clear glaze, covering over with a coat of transparent clear glaze.

Colors of this set may be used and fired into your pottery in your own kitchen oven, since a heat of no more than 300° F. is required to fuse the glaze. When several coats are being applied to obtain an opaque effect, the first four coats should be placed in a cold oven, which is then brought to a heat of 250°, and the piece is fired for a period of half an hour. After this, additional coats may be added, and the final firing in your oven should require an additional hour.

## CERAMIC POWDERS ON GLAZED WARES

The craftman seeking a most profes-

**SIMPLE SWEDISH DESIGN**
For designs on this jar, select your own colors from the
Swedish preferences described in Chapter 3.

bright gold and liquid bright silver also mature at this same temperature and are often used in combination with overglaze decoration. After a little practice, overglaze colors are easy to apply and by blending and shading they form an ideal medium for fine color detail.

Overglaze colors are used in large volume for decorating domestic dinnerware. In the studio pottery, overglaze or china painting colors, as they are often referred to, are used for painting china, tiles, ceramic jewelry and, in fact, artware of all kinds. Many artists buy pottery blanks (plain glaze ware), either in the dinnerware or artware line, and decorate by hand-painting with overglaze colors in their studios. This kind

sional touch generally prefers to use ceramic powders. In working with glazed tile or pottery, overglaze or china painting colors are used. The overglaze colors are painted or sprayed on ware which has already been glazed and fired. In other words, they are applied over another higher fired glaze, hence their name "overglaze." They then have to be fired in a kiln to their maturing temperature of 1375° F., to produce the finished product with its permanent retention of your color and design. ("Mature," in this sense, means to develop their true color.)

You can get a wide and delicate color range in the overglaze series. Liquid

**FOR A LADY**
On a potpourri jar for a lady, rose and leaves form an appropriate decoration.

of decoration does not require much equipment, and many a homemaker has found that her talent and experience in decorating her own pottery gave her a chance to turn the craft into a profitable business.

For hand painting, the color is mixed in a fat oil and turpentine medium. For mixing, you need a flat, smooth, hard surface, preferably a glass slab, and a steel spatula. Some color is placed on your mixing surface. Enough fat oil is added to dampen but not wet the color. Mix the powder ceramic paint with the spatula, then add turpentine until you get a mixture which will flow from a camel's-hair brush with ease. The mixture should be about the consistency of

**A BORDER DOES IT**

A simple border design—of Indian origin, in this case— is effective on a round object like the coffee pot shown.

thick cream (coffee cream—not whipping cream). A little practice will soon enable you to get the proper proportion. If the mixture needs more turpentine, the color will not flow from the brush. If you have too much turpentine, it will be runny on the ware. The addition of extra fat oil will improve the workability, but if too much fat oil is used it might cause blistering when the color is fired.

Thorough mixing of the powdered paint, using a rubbing and grinding action of the spatula, will break all fine lumps and improve workability. If you have a quantity of the mixture left at the end of the day, it can be stored for

**SWEDISH COFFEE POT**

On a coffee pot of clay, this interesting Swedish design is easy to paint and can be as dramatic as the colors you choose.

**DECORATE THE OLD PITCHER**
Flowers and leaves in the Swedish style,
plus bright colors, make an old object
new and decorative.

future use. It will thicken somewhat, but can be thinned down with turpentine.

## CERAMIC POWDERS ON UNGLAZED WARES

If you are working with unglazed pottery or tile—called "bisque" or "biscuit" ware—you use underglaze colors. These are applied to bisque ware and are then covered with a clear transparent glaze and fired under the glaze.

Underglaze colors have no maturing temperature of their own but mature (that is, develop their true color) at the maturing temperature of the transparent glaze used. The composition of the glaze has some effect on the color devel-

oped. In fact, some glazes might destroy some of the colors completely, as a result of the chemical reaction during the firing.

### How to Apply Underglaze Colors

There are several ways of applying underglaze colors and several mediums which can be used. For the home craftsman, hand painting, and the use of sevco gum and water as a medium, is recommended. Mix a small amount of underglaze color and water on a glass slab with a spatula. For every five parts of color and water mixed add approximately one part of sevco gum which is the consistency of rubber cement. Corn syrup may be substituted for sevco gum, if desired. This will give the mixture "body" and permit easy painting of the colors on the ware. Underglaze colors should be applied very thinly. If applied too heavily, the glaze will crawl off, leaving bare spots. A little practice is necessary to learn the proper thickness of application.

Another common source of trouble is too heavy application of glaze over the colors, especially on a vertical surface. If the glaze is applied too heavily, it might move or run during the firing and will pull the underglaze colors with it, producing a streaked effect. Therefore, it is advised that you practice on some discarded pieces, if any are available, before attempting to decorate one of your prize pieces. After you have mastered the art, however, you can produce some beautiful effects in multicolored ware. You can use white underglaze by itself or for mixing with other colors to produce pastel shades.

In mixing your ceramic paint, remember that you are working with a strong mineral oxide. A small speck of powder will supply a great amount of color. In the use of powdered ceramic paint, you are limited to the colors supplied by the manufacturers—it is not possible to mix two colors of ceramic paint powder to get an exact duplication of the colors shown in the color chart in Chapter 1. Your selection will have to come as close as the ceramic paint manufacturers' line permits to the colors recommended here. Mix only enough of the powdered ceramic paint for your immediate needs; the mixture quickly dries, and it will become useless if not applied quickly.

**BIRDS OF THE PUEBLO INDIANS**

Chapter 3 presented pictures of many different birds. Try a band of them on a bowl. The shape shown is easily decorated. Use two strips of masking tape to establish the wide band against which the bird drawings are to appear, after you have marked guide points with your ruler. Fill in the edges of tape with your paintbrush. White would make an excellent background for design figures in black.

If you are working with unglazed tile, pour water on the tile before starting to paint, as the tiles absorb any bit of moisture rapidly.

Do not be surprised that the ceramic paints appear rather bright. Once they have been applied to the tile, they will fade in the course of the firing. Reds and yellows are particularly subject to fading when the tile is baked in the kiln. For this reason, blues and greens are apt to be more satisfactory for the beginner as main color motifs.

### Applying the Design

Your first step in applying the design is to copy it on the tile with pencil—either by use of carbon paper from a

**BIRDS FROM PERU**

Birds follow each other around a pottery bowl in this Peruvian design that is reduced to essentials.

**PAINTING AN OVER-ALL PATTERN**

Bowls of the shape shown above are sometimes difficult to decorate without resorting to an over-all pattern. This Sioux Indian border design adaptation is easy to make if you divide the surface areas and measure carefully your space division. You can combine a number of colors in this pattern.

sketch sheet, or by freehand drawing. For the beginner, it is best to work from a sketch sheet, working out the designs as described in Chapter 2, or tracing from the illustrations in this book.

As we have indicated, it is advisable to have a few extra tiles to do a little experimental painting, when you make your first effort at painting on tile. The tile absorbs the paint with surprising speed. Ceramic paints may be washed off before they are thoroughly dry—or designs may be "erased" with turpentine.

When finished, the tiles will not take long to dry. But they will smear easily and you must handle them with the greatest care until they have been fired in a kiln—then they'll last forever. Allow the tiles twenty-four hours to dry before touching them—then take them to a nearby kiln for firing. You'll be able to find out from your phone book or hobby dealer, where the nearest kiln is located.

If you have worked with unglazed tile, the kiln people spray a glaze over your design, and the glaze and firing of

188

# Put Color on Your Table

Your dining will be more delightful with a decorated salad bowl and pottery pieces. Napkin clips too take cheerfully to color and design, as does the cake plate at lower right (but don't decorate on the cutting side).

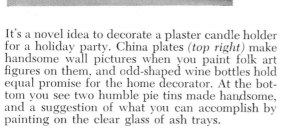

# Things You Can Decorate
# to Brighten Up the Home

It's a novel idea to decorate a plaster candle holder for a holiday party. China plates *(top right)* make handsome wall pictures when you paint folk art figures on them, and odd-shaped wine bottles hold equal promise for the home decorator. At the bottom you see two humble pie tins made handsome, and a suggestion of what you can accomplish by painting on the clear glass of ash trays.

**MEASURE IT CAREFULLY**

The design shown on this pottery bowl is done with a combination of ruler and French curve. You can make the zigzag line with your ruler. The other parts of the design can be sketched into position with your French curve once the basic areas have been carefully measured and indicated. A color plan might include cream, light red, and black.

the design into the clay are all accomplished in a single operation. If you have worked with glazed tile, of course, only the firing of the design into the clay is required.

## PHOTOGRAPHS ON TILE

For a novel use of decoration on tile, it is possible to have a reproduction in tile of a photographic print of your child, dog, horse, or any scene dear to your heart. Your glossy print is made into a lithographic stone and printed on glazed tile, using ceramic pigment instead of ink. The tile is varnished before the print is laid on. The kiln in which the tile is fired, burns away the paper at 800° F. and the color then goes into the glaze.

## FOR AUTOGRAPH FANS

A novel hobby is followed by an autograph fan from Jackson Heights, New York, who gets celebrities to sign their names with a china marking pencil on unglazed tiles which she furnishes

### FROM THE SWEDISH

An attractive decoration can be made by repeating flowers at intervals around a bowl, with or without other elements in the design.

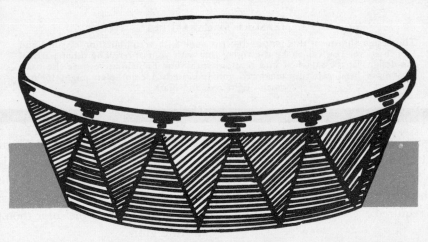

### GEOMETRIC PATTERN

To make this design, take the measurement of the lower edge of the molding which rims the top of the bowl. Decide how many triangles you want in the over-all design pattern, and divide the length of the molding into equal parts, marking off points on the rim. Do the same on the base of the bowl, as shown. Now, with pencil and ruler, draw in your lines. Brush-stroke over the penciled lines, and add the freehand brush strokes on the molding over the peak of each triangle.

for the purpose. These pencils are available in varied colors, at stationery stores. It is not necessary to have tiles baked when this special type of pencil is used, but our autograph collector does so in the interest of permanence.

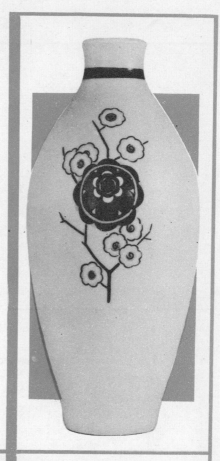

(Top)

**FLOWERS ON A VASE**

On a long, slender vase, the design is also long and slender. (You can adapt your own flowers from Chapter 2, or trace these.) Note the simple border around the neck of the vase.

(Left)

**PUEBLO INDIAN BOWL**

On a white ground, designs appear in black and red on the neck of this bowl, in black on the body.

CHAPTER 8

# It's Fun to
# PAINT on GLASS

Painting on glass offers you a world of easy, pleasurable adventures in self-expression. Your scope is wide—bottles, vases, pitchers, drinking glasses, dishes, doors, and other glass objects and surfaces of every shape and size gain enormously in charm and novelty under the magic influence of color and design. Complicated methods that require the skilled craftsman's hand and costly equipment, we shall pass over here—we shall show you only enjoyable ways of decorating glassware that anyone can follow with success.

One of the simplest and most appealing touches I have ever seen in glass decoration was achieved by a young hostess I know. She served a dinner at which the drinking glass of each guest bore his name, applied in water color to the outer surface of the glass, and fixed in place with colorless nail polish. She used a fine sable brush, and moistened the brush only slightly.

You can obtain an equally attractive result with decorative designs planned for more enduring use, with oil paints. For this you will need tube oil paints in colors indicated on the color chart in Chapter 1; 1/16- and 1/8-inch flat sable brushes; and 3/16-inch round sable brush; spar varnish; turpentine; Scotch or masking tape; tracing paper.

If you're working with a glass tumbler, simply trace your chosen design onto the tracing paper, and fasten the paper on the inner surface of a cleaned and dusted glass, facing out. Mix your colors on a palette—an old plate or saucer will do. Add a drop or two of varnish to each color, and thin with turpentine to the consistency of heavy cream. You should mix enough of each color to complete the painting of each object, as it is difficult to match shades when mixing more paint. If you have mixed too much, you may keep the paint fresh when not in use by sub-

**INITIALS ON A GLASS**

These tall letters strike a properly sophisticated note for an Old-fashioned glass. Gold would be suitable for the color of the decoration. For varied alphabets and monograms, see Chapter 4.

merging the palette in a pan of cold water.

Apply your paint sparingly, filling in the large areas first and adding details and outlines later, and taking care not to smear the paint as you work. Before you change from one color to another, clean your brushes in turpentine and wash them in soap and water.

After the piece is completed, allow the painted design to dry for two weeks. Then cover the design only, with clear varnish.

## NEW WAYS TO PAINT GLASS

Some special preparations are available for decorating glassware. You will find it helpful to employ some of the

**THIS DESIGN IS INFORMAL**

Suit the decoration to the purpose by painting this Pennsylvania Dutch rooster on an Old-fashioned glass.

**AZTEC BIRD DESIGN**

This quaint-looking bird may be painted in any colors you choose. Try others from Chapter 3.

Immerable are the different objects of glass that will gain in attractiveness if you decorate them. This illustration suggests some of the possibilities for your brush—drinking glasses, dishes, jars, vases, salt and pepper shakers, bottles. And the ornamentation can be as simple or as elaborate as your skill permits—note the light wavy lines on the jars in the foreground, easy adaptations of borders pictured in earlier chapters.

techniques which have been developed to improve your results.

A transparent mix added to colors can give a lovely translucent stained-glass effect.

For obtaining transparent colors, use a quick, one-stroke technique (described as the "free brush" technique). For an opaque, or glossy effect, load your brush with the coloring and use a slow and deliberate brush stroke. Then add a thin coat of the same coloring, thus covering over any brush marks.

For an etched effect, apply your coloring thinly; then, before it has dried, cut etched lines into the design with the pointed end of your brush or with another sharp object.

In applying your coloring, it is best to outline the area of a particular color

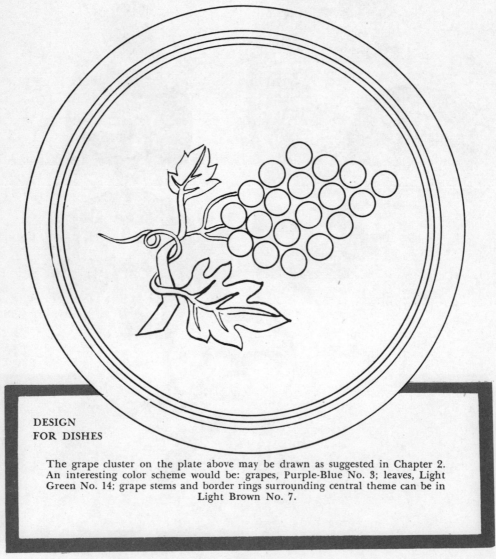

**DESIGN
FOR DISHES**

The grape cluster on the plate above may be drawn as suggested in Chapter 2. An interesting color scheme would be: grapes, Purple-Blue No. 3; leaves, Light Green No. 14; grape stems and border rings surrounding central theme can be in Light Brown No. 7.

with the small brush, allowing it to set. This serves as a "retaining wall" to hold in the color fill which you apply evenly, and with less danger of "running."

## LIQUID GLAZE ON GLASS

A new medium which offers an easy method of applying designs to glass is the plastic liquid glaze. It can be applied with equal ease to glass, chinaware, ceramics and metals. Liquid glaze, oven-fired in your own kitchen, will not suffer from washing in hot soapy dishwater, resists cigarette heat and is not affected by the use of alcohol in or on your glassware. It will not chip or peel.

The glaze comes in sets, complete with colors, clear glaze, reducer, and glazing brush.

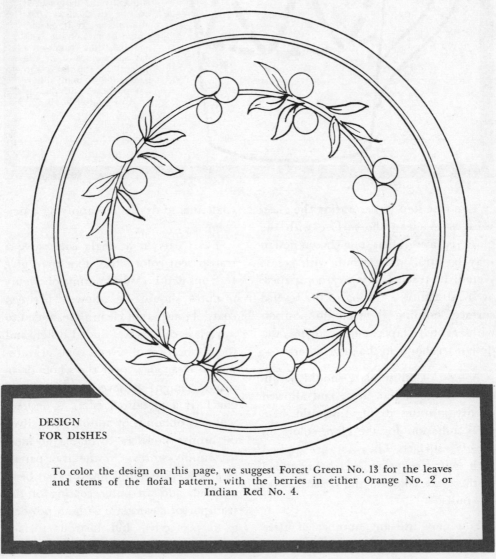

DESIGN
FOR DISHES

To color the design on this page, we suggest Forest Green No. 13 for the leaves and stems of the floral pattern, with the berries in either Orange No. 2 or Indian Red No. 4.

**BAND OF HEARTS**

Showing a favorite subject of Pennsylvania Dutch art in a broken-line treatment. Naturally the design need not be used on a glass mug alone—try it on any round object, or use it as a straight-line border on a flat surface. Most of the designs in this book can be adapted to many different purposes with hardly any trouble at all.

The first step in decorating the glassware is to clean the surface with the glaze reducer. Then your chosen design may be applied freehand, with grease pencil; by tracing, using carbon paper; or by attaching a tracing to the reverse surface, holding it firmly in position with Scotch tape, and copying the design freehand in the glaze colors.

A base of white glaze should be applied to the design area, and allowed twenty minutes drying time; the base gives adhesion for the glaze colors on the glass surface. The colors are applied with swift strokes, reducer being added to the glaze colors if the brush streaks or "pulls."

You may use any number of glaze colors in successive coats, giving each coat time to dry before applying a new color.

Two coats in a single color give a transparent color effect; four coats give lustrous depth. A drying time of twenty minutes should be allowed between coats. Transparent clear glaze, added to any glaze color, gives added luster, and the application of several coats of transparent clear glaze over the whole decorative design achieves a high-luster effect. If a metalized effect is desired, you may obtain it by adding gold, silver or bronze powders—available at most art supply stores — to the transparent clear glaze; after this mixture has been applied, add an outer coating of the transparent clear glaze without powder, as a protective and lustrous surface coating.

## GAME BIRDS ON GLASSES

You can put your hobbies on glass as well as on furniture and other things. The sportsman will find a set of glasses decorated with game birds an attractive addition to his party equipment. It would be best to use authentic coloring for the kinds of birds shown.

The glaze reducer is used to remove portions of your design which you may wish to correct—if you make the change before firing the piece in your oven. Simply moisten a clean cloth with it, and wipe away that part of the design you wish to change. The reducer is also used to thin the glaze if it thickens while standing, and to clean the brushes. Be sure that the brush is cleaned completely after each color has been applied, before starting on the use of another color.

## Firing

The most attractive feature in the use of the plastic liquid glaze on glassware, pottery or chinaware is that the colors may be made permanent by firing in your own kitchen oven. This plastic does not require the tremendous heat which is demanded in the use of ceramic powders or paints on pottery. Your problem, in fact, is to be certain that your oven does not reach a temperature over 300° F. You should have a good oven thermometer, in satisfactory working condition, and check frequently to see that the heat is not exceeded. Otherwise, your colors will change under the greater temperature, or bubbles may form in the glaze.

If you are seeking a solid effect in coloring your glass or chinaware, and have therefore planned to use more than four coats of glaze, give your decorated pieces an intermediate firing after the fourth coat. Put the piece in a cold oven, increasing it slowly to 250° or 300°. Leave the piece in for half an hour, and then add the other coats of glaze.

When the piece is ready for final

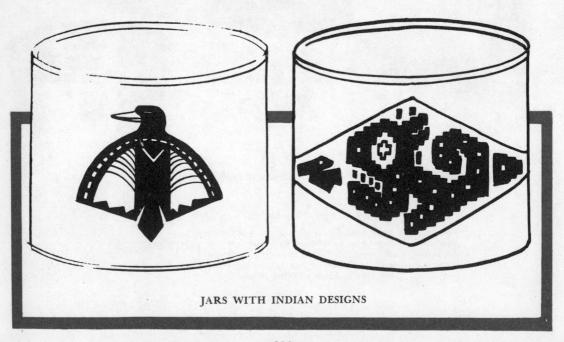

JARS WITH INDIAN DESIGNS

## WHITE DESIGN ON FLOWER VASE

This design will be effective in white on plain glass, with the vertical borders of dots painted in freehand. The sides which are too narrow for the birds to be repeated are decorated with a rhythmic leaf pattern and the flowers reduced in size.

**MAKE HIGHBALL GLASSES GAY**

Illustrating some ways you can run designs around glasses. The patterns
may run up and down, or in wavy lines rather than in simple, straight
bands.

firing—either with less than four coats, or with a greater number of coats of glaze and an intermediate firing—place it in a cold oven. The firing process will cause the glaze to fuse into a sparkling and durable finish. The final firing requires an hour at the maximum heat (300° F.). If the piece is left in the oven

**WINE BOTTLES ARE DECORATIVE**

Wine bottles in unusual shapes become ornamental knick-knacks when you decorate them with small designs like these. Paint the designs in several different colors.

for somewhat over an hour, the durability of the finish is increased.

If, through failure to follow directions in applying glaze, small bubbles or blisters appear on the glassware after firing, you may use very fine sandpaper to remove these blemishes. Then reglaze the piece.

203

**THISTLE
IN OVER-ALL PATTERN**

You can draw this flower freehand, or trace and enlarge it readily by following the instructions in this chapter and Chapter 2. The tiny crosses in an appropriate color give a pleasing over-all effect.

## REVERSE PAINTING ON GLASS

One of the most attractive ornamental practices of the artistic-minded craftsmen in the Pennsylvania German communities was the development of reverse painting on glass. The glass faces of grandfather clocks and framed mirrors were ornamented with floral patterns, sketches of homes, human figures, hunting scenes, etc.

### Materials Needed

To apply your choice in decorative designs to modern pieces—to the glass top of a coffee table, glass ash trays, glass cabinet doors, dressing-table mirror borders, etc.—the following are needed:

Oil paints, in colors indicated in the color chart, as you may require; one tube of flat white ground in Japan; 3/16-inch sable brush for outlining; 3/8-inch square shader for small spaces; 3/4-inch square shader for skies and foreground; India ink; clear varnish, turpentine; compass; fine compass pen; steel ruler for squaring edges; tracing paper; fine drawing pencil; Scotch tape or masking tape.

Enamel paints may also be used for reverse painting on glass.

### Tracing and Painting

Trace your decorative design on tracing sheet, scaled to the size of your decorative glass piece, using fine pencil. Attach your tracing to the reverse side of your glass piece with the Scotch or masking tape. Now, on the outer surface of your glass, outline your design, using the India ink. When this has dried, you are ready to turn over your glass and apply your reverse painting. It is well to indicate on your original tracing the colors to be used in each area, and to refer to this constantly and carefully as you work.

Mix your tube oil paints with a small quantity of varnish, and thin with turpentine. First draw all the outlines—

**EASY DESIGNS ON GLASSES**

A flower, a bird, leaves—with such easy designs a plain drinking glass can become an object in the colorful tradition of folk art.

Try some of the patterns in Chapter 2 on your glassware, and use bright colors on them.

generally these will be in black or brown. Take care to insure delicate lines, with even-flowing freehand brush strokes. Paint with one color at a time. Set the glass aside (preferably where it will be kept free from dust) to dry—thirty-six hours may do, but a week is better assurance. Then back the entire surface with a coat of flat white, if desired, thinned with turpentine, adding a second coat twenty-four hours later.

Among the more novel pieces of decorated glassware I have seen is an old brass kerosene headlamp from a 1907 Oldsmobile, now hanging as a plant container from an old brass weathervane affixed to the wall of a Washington, D. C., residence. A brass chain is suspended from the weathervane to hold the old headlamp, whose frame and top are highly polished. Inside the headlamp is a flowerpot containing an ivy plant, whose stems cascade groundward through the opened glass door.

The two side panels of glass, however, are brightly decorated with designs in colors which set off the green of the ivy plant.

## ADVANCED PAINTING ON GLASS

Hand coloring of glassware, as practiced by the experts, is a complicated art, and takes years of practice for success. Colors used are fine powdered glasses, applied with brush or pen, and fused into the surface of the glass at 2700 degrees temperature in a long oven with a moving floor, called an annealing lehr. The decoration thus becomes an integral part of the glass and cannot be removed. The powdered glass colors, mixed with special oils, that are used in this hand decorating, change hue completely under heat, and only the craftsman experienced with their use can tell beforehand how they will come out.

# CHAPTER 9

# COLORING FABRICS
# To Your Fancy

If you enjoy color in everyday living, decorating fabrics will hold a powerful appeal for you. With the aid of color and design you can add a striking personal note not only to your linens and home furnishings, but to your clothing and accessories as well. The fabrics you use may be as inexpensive as you wish —your own touch in decoration will give them quality and distinction. The procedures to follow involve the use of textile colors, or oil paints, and they are simple and practical.

Some of the designs and arrangements which are easy and fun to do are illustrated in this chapter for your guidance. Of course, you will want to change many of them to represent your own personal ideas and the colors which best fit your own taste and needs.

Perhaps you have a favorite wallpaper with a particularly distinctive, colorful design pattern. You can easily reproduce this theme in your draperies, bedspread, or slipcovers. You can individualize your linen with your own monogram or initials, or make them

**DECORATE YOUR LINENS**

Plain white handkerchiefs, napkins, and other linens become possessions uniquely your own when you decorate them with designs of your choosing.

more interesting by applying a motif from the design of your china.

Even your plainest costume can be made smartly different by the repetition of a simple color design on your accessories—hat, bag, purse, belt or gloves. Accessories designed to match the ornamentation of your costume help to make it outstandingly attractive.

Children's clothes can be made particularly appealing with perky little designs, initials or names in color.

Here are some of the things you may want to decorate:

*Bath*
Guest towels
Curtains
Bath mats

*Kitchen*
Towels
Table mats
Paper-and-string bag
Curtains
Potholders

*Bedroom*
Dresser scarfs
Curtains
Pillow cases
Chair covers
Sheets to match
Bedspreads
Shoe bag
Laundry bag

*Living Room*
Drapes
Doilies
Valances
Bridge sets
Curtain tie-backs
Pillow tops
Footstool covers
Slipcovers
Arm rests
Head rests

*Dining Room*
Scarfs
Table linen
Drapes
Place mats
Chair covers
Tray cloths

*Feminine Accessories*
Bed jackets
Dresses
Blouses
Smocks
Knitting bag
Sports jackets
Beach bags
Gloves
Aprons
Night gowns
Slips
Sun bonnets
Socks
Beach robes
Skirts
Hose
Cuff and collars
Belts
Pocketbooks
Dickies
Scarfs
Handkerchiefs
Hats

*Man*
Shirts (initials)
Ties
Handkerchiefs
Pajamas
Sports shirts

*Miscellaneous*
Portfolio covers
Phone book cover
Scrap book cover
Auto seat cover
Pennants
Canvas lawn chairs

*Child*
Pinafore and dress
Hair ribbons
Sun suits
Pocketbooks
Kimonos
Dolls
Doll blankets
Bibs

## STARTING WITH TEXTILE COLORS

Textile colors come ready-mixed and packed in sets. Available at hobby and department stores, these sets provide all the equipment you need to hurry you along in your adventures in fabric decorating.

To begin the job of color decorating on fabrics, first select one of the cut stencils that are provided in the set of textile colors, and do a little experimenting. This will prove such fun and so easy that you will be eager to proceed to the next step. And that step should be tracing some design or some pattern around the house that appeals to you strongly—perhaps from a slipcover, an old dress print, or one of the designs illustrated in this book.

You can make a stencil of it yourself by following the procedure described a little later in this chapter.

## AFTERNOON TEA SERVICE

Attractive floral decorations such as these are easy to apply by stenciling with textile colors.

## Hints for Combining Colors

To achieve attractive color combinations is not difficult. You simply follow the recommendations outlined in Chapter 1. Two or three colors will be ample for an interesting color effect. There are, of course, many thousands of colors from nature from which to make a selection. However, the colors represented in Chapter 1 provide a good starting point to help you develop your color schemes.

Tints may be made by adding a special material called extender which comes with your set. Color and shades may be created by adding black. To gray a color, all you need to do is make it less intense, adding either black or extender to achieve this purpose. Remember, gray colors combined with full-strength colors help to give you fine subdued color effects. Remember too, that the selection of the right color is most important and above all, every color in a design must be balanced to make the effect pleasing to the eye. If one color stands out like a sore thumb, the effect cannot be harmonious.

The best rule to follow is this: Use bright colors only in small spots; for large areas use only tints (light colors), shades (dark colors), or grayed variations of the colors you choose. A small spot of color will serve to balance a larger area of weakened color.

Certain colors attract the eye more readily than others, even though they may be equally intense. Yellow, orange and red are colors of this type. They demand and get more attention than greens or blues.

Nature follows an effective rule by displaying a bright red or yellow flower against a mass of green foliage. Imagine the result if the colors were reversed.

## How to Cut Stencils

Stenciling is such an easy process—even if you've never been introduced to a stencil you'll be friends in short order. We have advised you to begin with one of the ready-cut stencils that you find in your textile color set. Later, when you cut your own stencil, follow these rules:

*If it is a one-color stencil:*

1. Fasten the stencil paper (it comes with your set, or you may obtain it at any art supply store) to the design with tape or thumb tacks.

2. Trace the design with a hard pencil. Stay on the lines.

3. Cut the stencil on the lines with a stencil cutter, sharp knife or razor blade.

*If it is a design of more than one color:*

1. Draw a right angle, or put two pieces of tape or pins at right angles, where the upper left corner of your stencil paper falls. Always place your stencil so that the upper left corner fits into this. For borders, use a strip of paper or cardboard as a guide.

2. Trace outlines for each color on a separate piece of stencil paper.

3. Place stencils together and hold up to the light to be sure the various parts of your design fall into place.

# DESIGN IDEAS FOR CLOTHES AND HOME FURNISHINGS

The three designs in this picture represent the one-color type of stenciling.

DESIGN IDEAS FOR CLOTHES AND HOME FURNISHINGS

Flower and leaf motifs in two separate stencils combine in a finished
design of varied color and shading.

# DESIGN IDEAS FOR CLOTHES AND HOME FURNISHINGS

Intricate three-color stencil patterns which will give scope to your color preferences.

# DESIGN IDEAS FOR CLOTHES AND HOME FURNISHINGS

Three stencils of flower and leaf show how easy-to-make motifs join in a simple pattern which still has ample variety.

## Steps in Stenciling

1. Eliminate all size or filler, as it is sometimes called, from the fabric material you are planning to use. This is done by washing in warm, soapy water, rinsing thoroughly, and then pressing.

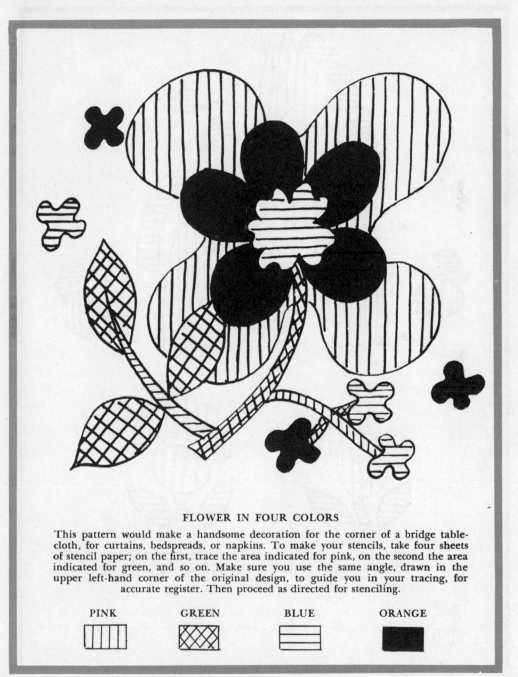

### FLOWER IN FOUR COLORS

This pattern would make a handsome decoration for the corner of a bridge table-cloth, for curtains, bedspreads, or napkins. To make your stencils, take four sheets of stencil paper; on the first, trace the area indicated for pink, on the second the area indicated for green, and so on. Make sure you use the same angle, drawn in the upper left-hand corner of the original design, to guide you in your tracing, for accurate register. Then proceed as directed for stenciling.

| PINK | GREEN | BLUE | ORANGE |
|------|-------|------|--------|

2. Mix your colors. To every color, add extender. The colors will penetrate the fabric better. Extender also serves to make a color lighter. If you want it darker, add black (a little goes a long way).

BLUE

PINK

**DESIGN IN TWO COLORS**
Suitable for towels or napkins, this design requires only two stencils.

# STENCILING MADE EASY

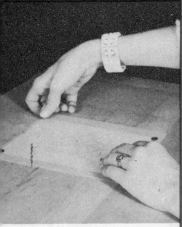

. Tack stencil paper over the sheet
n which your design appears.

B. Trace design onto stencil paper.

C. Cut stencil, using stencil cutter,
sharp knife or single-edge razor
blade.

). For two-color design, establish a
uide point with pins so that you
an place stencil paper for each
olor in position accurately.

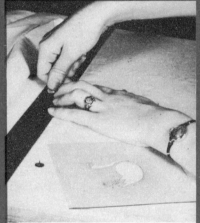

E. Use a strip of paper or guide
board as a guide for side borders to
help insure accuracy in placing
stencil sheet for each color correctly.

F. Mix your colors and extender or
black.

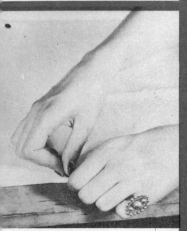

G. Attach your fabric to a smooth
urface, such as a drawing board or
heavy cardboard.

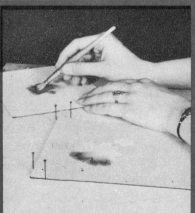

H. Work color carefully into brush
before applying to fabric. Get rid of
excess paint by running brush across
paper or scrap of cloth.

I. In applying color, let the brush
touch the stencil sheet ½ inch from
the painting, sweeping across the
opening with your brush stroke.

3. Place a white blotter under the fabric, to absorb excess color. Stretch the washed, pressed, and dried fabric tightly over the surface you are going to work on (a drawing board or large piece of cardboard is excellent). Fasten the fabric down with Scotch tape or thumb tacks.

4. Place the stencil in position on the cloth.

5. Stir your colors. Work the color into the brush, then stroke across a cloth or paper to remove excess color. Remember you need very little color on your brush. It is decidedly better to use several light applications of color on the fabric rather than one heavy coating.

6. Allow your brush to hit the stencil about one-half inch from the opening and sweep across the opening, always toward the center. Repeat the stroke until you have the desired intensity of color. Work the color into the fabric with firm strokes.

7. Dry thoroughly. Do not set the colors until the design has dried for at least twelve hours. A twenty-four-hour drying period is better, even though the colors will appear dry in a few minutes. Your attention to this simple detail will increase the durability of your work.

8. "Set" the colors with a hot iron. The "setting" of textile colors is simplicity itself. When dry (see step 7 above), place a cloth over the face of the design and iron for at least one minute with a hot iron (350° F.). Turn the fabric over and repeat the process. For rayon use a warm iron (200°-230° F.) for a longer period. After the colors have been "set," a dampened pressing cloth may be used as desired.

## Other Uses of Textile Colors

If you enjoy stenciling with textile colors, you may want to go on to other craft applications for which this versatile medium is so well suited. For a speedy way to repeat a design a great number of times, the silk screen process is a good idea. Silk screen kits are available for this work.

The craft worker with a special flair for hand blocking can use this process with textile colors. If you are at all experienced with the air brush, you may choose to work with it in this medium. You may also apply the colors freehand, following the basic rules given for applying color with stencils.

## OIL PAINTS ON FABRIC

Ordinary artists' oil paint in tubes is also an excellent medium for decorating textiles. It is quite easy to use in freehand painting. Moreover, oil-painted fabrics can be washed without damaging the decoration.

### Materials Needed

Besides oil paints, you require a flat ½-inch sable brush to apply them to large areas, and a round ¼-inch sable watercolor brush for smaller areas. Rectified spirits of turpentine, vinegar, carbon paper, tracing paper, etc., are also needed.

**IMITIVE AND COLORFUL**—This design, featuring oversized leaves and wild strawberries, is repeated over large
eas. Your color scheme might be: white background, Light Green No. 14 leaves, Light Yellow No. 9 shadow surrounding leaves, Dark Brown No. 5 stem and leaf veins, and Dark Blue No. 15 strawberries.

**INSETTIA DESIGN**—The large poinsettia motif is in outline, partially overlapping an irregularly-shaped background
ure. Fabric is colored Ivory No. 10, background for flower is Rose No. 19, outline of flower and leaf is black, center of
flower is Light Yellow No. 9, background of leaf is Light Green No. 14.

SPOUTING WHALE—A border design of a spouting whale above waves in an over-all pattern makes a gay decoration. Of course you can use any colors that suit your fancy. The brighter the hues the better, especially if you use this design on curtains or a bedspread in the child's room.

A LIVELY DESIGN—Representing a Pennsylvan[ia] Dutch cock in a frame-within-frame setting, this desi[gn] is bold and lively looking. Suggested colors are: ba[ck?] Ivory No. 10; frame outlining cock, Silver Gray No. [ ] circle on inside of frame, Forest Green No. 15; acce[nt?] color under wings and feet, both Indian Red No. [ ]

Repeat a design theme on several objects that go together like this flower and leaf pattern on water tumbler, place mats, and napkins.

# Designs
# from Nature
# on Fabric

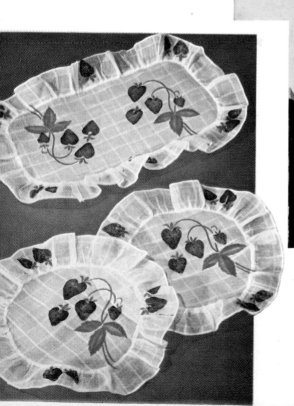

It's easy to stencil lovely designs on fabric pieces like the luncheon cloth and napkins above, or the dainty, ruffled place mats below (whose strawberry theme might be repeated on kitchen curtains).

# Fabrics . . .

Pennsylvania Dutch designs of tulips, birds, and hearts go well on a place mat, too *(top right)*. This one has been cut from cork. The luncheon cloth below it displays stenciled designs of a Mexican boy and girl.

A pear and berry pattern and child's name decorate place mats and drinking glass *(above)*. The same design might be carried over to canisters. Three bibs and a cork place mat *(left)* show you colorful designs that will please the very young. These same patterns will brighten up nursery furniture and walls.

### FLOWER IN A FRAME

Note how effective this ornament is on a rough-textured fabric. The cloth is white, the frame is Silver Gray No. 18, the flower Orange No. 2, the center of the flower and the stem are Forest Green No. 13.

PINEAPPLE DESIGN—This two-toned pineapple design illustrates an effective contrast of light and dark color values. A stencil for the pineapple can be cut from a folded piece of light cardboard—when you unfold it, the entire pineapple will appear. Your color scheme might be: Light Blue No. 16 and Light Green No. 14.

## Preparing the Cloth and Design

Your first step is to iron out the fabrics with which you intend to work. Then you are ready to trace your design.

Spread out the piece to be decorated on a hard flat surface to determine the proper position of the design. Space designs as evenly and carefully as possible. Then mark the exact position of each design by placing a few small dots along the outer edges of the design. In this way you can correct any mistake before it is too late.

Trace design onto tracing paper. Then place tracing paper and carbon paper on the fabric, carbon face down. Trace designs — the carbon will carry the design onto the fabric.

## How to Paint

Oil paints should be thinned with "permanent mixture" (turpentine, oil of wintergreen and acetic acid) or rectified spirits of turpentine. Use only one color at a time when painting. An old plate will do as a palette for mixing your paints. Put a small amount of paint on the plate.

First put your brush in the paint thinner, then in the paint. The brush should be moistened with color enough to cover the paint brush bristles completely, but not so much that the paint will drip as the brush is held over the palette. Fill in all spaces for the one color on the fabric, brush-stroking very lightly so that the color doesn't run. Fill in all the areas on the entire fabric piece which call for the use of this color. Then go on to the next color.

Wash the brush thoroughly in turpentine after each color has been completely applied, before putting the next color on your palette.

Above all, avoid getting drops of paint splashed onto your cloth.

When all the painting is finished and allowed to dry, take a large clean white cloth, dipped in vinegar and wrung out; place it on the decorated material and press it over the fabric with a hot iron. This will "fix" your design and colors into the fabric material.

When an oil-painted fabric requires cleaning, wash with lukewarm suds. You may squeeze the piece, but do not wring it.

# CHAPTER 10

# Color and Design
# FOR YOUR ROOMS

So far we have been looking around the house at the many different things we can decorate—pottery, furniture, fabrics, tin, and all the wares and trappings that make a house a home. These, to borrow a word from the theater, are the "props" of our daily living. But what of the setting in which they appear? Walls, floors, doors, and the rest of the home scene emphatically provide worthwhile subjects for your art. They can gain enormously in warmth and charm if you apply color and decorative design in keeping with the purpose they are meant to serve.

Naturally, it is necessary to start with a plan—but what plan?

Some people will pick their colors on the simple "I-like-thus-and-so" basis; some will seek psychological expression through use of color and ornamental design; some will choose for durability, in deference to the smoke and soot which stain metropolitan residences;

some will use combinations suited to the multi-purpose room, others will use colors to change the apparent size and shape of the room. Some will match colors to the woodwork of the furniture, others will consider the daylight exposure of a room and base color selection upon this factor.

Many decorators will tell you to select a favorite painting, and to match the colors in the room to the colors on the canvas which dominates your wall. Others will start with the colors of the walls themselves, and relate all colors in the room to the wall color. Still others —a considerable percentage of your traditional decorators—will use the colors of flooring as a starting point, and select other interior colors in harmony.

Actually, it is not too important which is the starting premise upon which you select your room colors, either for furniture or for the decorative designs on painted furniture and

DRESS UP YOUR GARAGE

One or more hex signs and an "ever-growing" garden at the sides and back of the building create a note of cheer and original character. The garage might be painted in Silver Gray No. 18, Buff No. 8, Ivory No. 10, or white as a base color. Many of the design and color themes shown in this book would be equally appropriate.

ornamental ware.

The important part is to make a choice of such a starting point, and then plan accordingly.

## SELECTING COLORS AND DESIGNS

Get away from the old hackneyed colors — use green the color of jade, yellow the hue of butter. For fresh, new effects, accent your red with blue, your blue with green, your yellows with brown—lighten your colors with white.

There are so many points at which your individual character can be given free expression. From the outside of your home to the place cards at a formal dinner party, there are means of expressing yourself.

The Mennonites of Pennsylvania announced to the world that a marriageable daughter lived in a home by painting the door blue. I know a man who

painted the flagstones of the walk to his door blue, not explaining his motive until the job was done; a flurry of shyness in the family was overcome as the humor of it appealed even to the young lady in question.

The Pennsylvania Dutch could not leave a barn undecorated (and the barns often overshadowed the house in architectural splendor). As we have mentioned, huge "hex" signs in geometrical patterns were painted on the barns to ward off evil spirits. A few of these designs might not be out of place on your garage.

Is there a superstition in your household? Give voice to it—in full color.

If your little girl is fascinated by train rides, and by the whistle of the locomotive down the valley—let her have locomotives on the walls or floor of her room, on the dresser drawers, instead of the more traditional and less imaginative hearts and flowers.

## NEW ENGLAND BARN WITH PENNSYLVANIA DUTCH ACCENT

This barn at Assinippi, Massachusetts, exhibits on its doors and windows modern adaptations of old Pennsylvania Dutch designs. They are painted in vivid yellows, reds, blues, and greens, against a background of green so dark that it appears to be black. The designs were executed by W. Graham Law, who appears in the picture.

HEX SIGNS FOR DECORATING

These hex signs may be used for decorating the outside of your garage, house, or other buildings. You can supply your own color schemes—no need to follow those appearing elsewhere in this book. These outlines show the simplicity of the patterns, which may be reproduced with ruler, compass, and French curve.

Is your husband a poker addict? Decorate his closet door or the card-table cover with a five-ace hand—deuces wild!

Above all, don't be alarmed by the considerations presented in the selection of colors and decorative designs. Don't set out to discuss your plans with everyone—the number of different ideas and criticisms will make your head whirl.

Take your own good time to make up your mind about what you want; take time to check through the suggestions offered in these pages, the rules and the points to consider and the methods of proceeding with your design plans.

Then go to it! Set to work boldly,

freely, with confidence. You can't go wrong when you satisfy your own inherent good taste and judgment.

## DESIGNS FOR YOUR FLOORS

With painted floors, there is much greater scope for the ingenious and personalized use of color in starting "from the floor up" with a color plan. The variety of colors, patterns, harmonies and designs can be made to blend with any desired seasonal effect, however transient, and with gratifying effect both from the standpoint of appearance and of cost.

A painted floor can provide a suitable foil for any decorative purpose. It can substitute the design and the color elements ordinarily furnished by a rug, or it can provide attractive background treatment for carpet or rug.

## SPATTER-DASH FLOORS

Many early American homes had floors painted by the spatter-dash method, and this tradition is being revived in modern ones. It is especially well suited for playroom and porch floors. The great appeal of a spatter-dash floor lies in its colorful appearance and informality. Moreover, the technique is simplicity itself. It consists merely of applying to your floor an undercoat of flat paint and a foundation color, then spattering your other colors, and varnishing over.

### Selecting the Colors

In selecting colors for a spatter-dash floor, think of the room as a whole. The colors of any decorative feature in the room can be attractively enhanced by repeating some or all of the colors in the floor spatter. The spatter-dash treatment renders it comparatively easy to repeat any bright accent color used in a room.

Spatter-dash floor colors, like all others, should be selected with a view to effective color relationships, in keeping with directions given in Chapter 1. To insure a pleasing result, colors which do not harmonize should be avoided in spatter arrangements. Successful choice of colors will provide a grouping that blends appealingly when viewed from a short distance — eye

DESIGNS OF STARS AND PETALS

Experiments with the compass resulted in these designs, which are as appropriate as the hex signs for home decoration. Try creating some of your own designs with this simple tool.

height, for instance. The result should be an overall appearance of one color, pleasingly variegated.

It is usually best to apply a grayed or

very dark base color to serve as a foil for the bright accent tones of the actual spatter finish. If your floor has a flat finish, use either gloss or flat paints for spatters; if the background flooring is gloss (that is, if it is a varnished or shellac-finish flooring area), use flat paint spatters.

If you wish a spatter which will stand out, use only one bright color. The following table of color groupings will enable you to select the combination best suited for supplying the degree of contrast required; colors are listed in order of descending contrast:

| Foundation Color | Spatter Color |
|---|---|
| Black or dark brown | Yellow or cream |
| White | Blue-green, yellow-green or cream |
| White | Light or dark red |

For a really good black floor, first apply a vermilion ground coat, then cover with two coats of black, slightly tinted with Chinese blue.

Usually, it is the practice to mingle a number of harmonious accent colors in the spatter. Three is a safe minimum.

Experiment on a piece of lumber, cardboard or paper until you get the proportion of the colors to be used arranged to your liking before actually commencing the work.

It is safest for an amateur to keep spatter colors for floors closely related to the ground color. But this need not stop you from using a lighter spatter on a darker ground.

Here are some spatter color schemes suitable for areas indicated:

PORCH

| *Foundation Color:* | Dark Brown No. 5 |
|---|---|
| *Spatter 1:* | Light Brown No. 7 |
| *Spatter 2:* | Leaf Green No. 12 |

FRONT HALL

| *Foundation Color:* | Light Brown No. 7 |
|---|---|
| *Spatter 1:* | Buff No. 8 |
| *Spatter 2:* | Purple-Blue No. 3 or Light Blue No. 16 |

LIVING ROOM

| *Foundation Color:* | Dark Brown No. 5 |
|---|---|
| *Spatter 1:* | Light Brown No. 7 |
| *Spatter 2:* | Silver Gray No. 18 |
| *Spatter 3:* | Orange No. 2 |

KITCHEN

| *Foundation Color:* | Purple-Blue No. 3 |
|---|---|
| *Spatter 1:* | Light Blue No. 16 |
| *Spatter 2:* | Ivory No. 10 |

RECREATION ROOM or NURSERY

| *Foundation Color:* | Silver Gray No. 18 |
|---|---|
| *Spatter 1:* | Yellow No. 1 |
| *Spatter 2:* | Light Blue No. 16 |
| *Spatter 3:* | Light Yellow No. 9 |

Another combination that might look well in any room where green is the dominant note (for instance, the hall or living room or dining room) follows:

| *Foundation Color:* | Forest Green No. 13 |
|---|---|
| *Spatter 1:* | Leaf Green No. 12 |
| *Spatter 2:* | Buff No. 8 |
| *Spatter 3:* | Light Yellow No. 9 (this may be omitted) |

An interesting combination for a feminine bedroom or nursery might be:

| *Foundation Color:* | Rose No. 19 |
|---|---|
| *Spatter 1:* | Pink No. 17 |
| *Spatter 2:* | Silver Gray No. 18 |

To make this less bright, use such a combination as:

## SPATTER DESIGN WITH COLORED BORDER

In the center area of a room, this design has a rug-like effect. A border of one-inch width will separate the spatter area from the solid-color part of the flooring to the best effect. Note the painted chest in the background, with drawers in different colors and side panel matching the lower drawer.

*Foundation Color:* Maroon No. 6
*Spatter 1:* Rose No. 19
*Spatter 2:* Silver Gray No. 18

### Applying Spatter Color

The application process is easy. First, however, you would be well advised to try it on cellar stairs—or an old carton top — to familiarize yourself with the technique.

Equipment for spatter-dashing is very simple. All you require is an old paint brush, floor paint of a consistency somewhat heavier than is used for regular brushing, and a flat stick (or a ruler, table knife, sieve or strainer).

The spatter-dash effect can be applied as follows:

First, spread newspaper around the lower wall where it meets the floor, using masking tape to hold it in place and to protect the walls from spatter. Be sure to wear old clothing and a head covering!

Second, prepare the floor with an

229

undercoat of flat paint; when it is dry, apply a foundation color.

After this coat is dry, dip your brush in one of the bright accent colors you have selected and scrape the bristles of the brush with the edge of the stick or knife blade (if you use a sieve, bang the brush against it). Repeat this process over a strip of floor, then go back and do the same with one of the other colors. Cover the floor this way, completing one strip at a time; do not attempt to do one color at a time over the whole floor area.

To make the spatter small, hold the stick a foot from the floor and use less paint on the brush; to make larger spatter spots, hold the stick three feet from the floor and increase the amount of paint used on the brush.

Always buy a good quality of floor paint or deck enamel. If an old painted floor in good condition is to be repainted, you can paint directly over it, provided the new paint color is darker in value.

However, for best results, remove the old floor paint with a reliable paint remover and start fresh.

### A Border for the Spatter-Dash Floor

Decorative designs or patterns can be applied by stencils as a border for the spatter-dashed area. If this is to be done, it is well to cover that area with newspaper after the spatter-dash colors have dried. The colors used in the stenciled designs should, of course, repeat the colors appearing in the spatter-dash pattern.

## APPLYING A FLOOR DESIGN BY STENCIL

Stenciled designs in the form of borders or all-over repeated motifs—or a central decorative theme with border treatment—have wide appeal. We have explained how to cut stencils in Chapter 2. In applying stencils, it is necessary to hold your brush at right angles to the floor and tap the paint on. The finish coat selected for the basic floor paint should have a matte (eggshell) finish to enable the oil paint used for stenciling to take hold.

Traditional motifs are the easiest to use. Cut stencils of a size which will look best on the expanse of your floor—scale is an important consideration. If they are too small they will look insignificant; if they are too large they will make the room look smaller. The floor design can be repeated effectively on walls, furnishings, and on other objects if you will follow the methods described in earlier chapters.

When using a border, be certain to measure your space carefully, so you can lengthen or shorten each section of your pattern appropriately.

After you have stenciled the floor, and the paint is thoroughly dry, do not fail to apply a thick coat of wax or transparent varnish to prolong the life of your designs. If it is a kitchen floor, or any other which is subject to frequent soap-and-water scrubbing, spar varnish should be used.

## GEOMETRIC PATTERNS

On broad, even-width floor boards it is simple to work out geometrical patterns in two-tone color combinations. For best results, first treat the floor to the usual basic color finish, using a light-value color. Next, mark the design in chalk in squares, diamonds, or other designs the width of the boards. Give the darker areas in the design a coat of the darker color. The mechanically produced design patterns illustrated in this volume are also easy to follow and apply.

## NOVEL BORDERS

Border designs for floor treatment, harmonizing with a throw rug in the central area, can also provide a novel and enhancing effect for your room. A stippling effect may be obtained for a painted floor with a special stipple brush; another interesting effect is obtained by dipping a crumpled piece of paper into the paint and pressing it against the solid-color paint floor. If two or more colors are desired in using the latter process, they should all be applied together, completing one area of the floor without giving any of the colors time to dry.

## WALLPAPER ON FLOORS

A modern touch that is becoming increasingly popular is the use of wallpaper to provide a border for floor areas. Wallpaper may be applied effectively, too, for a small area under a glass-topped coffee table, where it will not be walked on and will show to good advantage through the glass surface.

It is necessary, of course, to have a flat-surfaced flooring to make such an application successful; a soft-wood flooring in poor condition would be likely to tear the paper. Regular wallpaper paste is used to apply the paper to the floor surface.

The first step in application should be a thorough cleansing of the floor area to be covered, and removal of any specks or splinters that might cause bulges or tears in the paper. A waterfast type of wallpaper should be used, but since this type has come to represent 90 per cent of the wallpaper printed, there is no great problem in getting a selection of patterns and colors suitable for your purpose.

The floor area to be covered with the wallpaper should be sized first. Use a cellulose sponge for applying the glue size to the floor. It takes but a few minutes to dry. Any excess can be removed with a damp cloth.

Next apply paste to the wallpaper and paste it to the floor. To remove air bubbles and paste stains from the surface, wipe over the paper with a damp cloth, pressing firmly to the floor.

When the paper is dry, size it with a covering liquid to seal its surface against absorption of the protective coatings of varnish. You thereby prevent the varnish from causing the wallpaper to change color.

The "sizing" material to use is a white shell glue, available at most hardware stores. All you need is a very small

This combination of a heart and simple flower forms is appropriate for a wall, or a panel on it. Note the balancing Pennsylvania Dutch eight-pointed stars in the lower corners. Put in your own name and the date.

| Color Combination | Mood | |
|---|---|---|
| 1. Silver-gray and chartreuse | Subtle | ..................... |
| 2. Violet and olive | Sophisticated | ......... |
| 3. Wine-red, vermilion and jade green | Tragic | .................... |
| 4. Dusty rose and deep grayed turquoise | Serious | ................... |
| 5. Tan and soft grayed blue | Novel | ..................... |
| 6. Grayed green and beige | Amusing | ................ |
| 7. Bright pink, bottle green and yellow | Pleasing | ................. |
| 8. Mustard yellow and violet | Discordant | ............. |

The correct answers are: Subtle (1); Sophisticated (5); Tragic (2); Serious (6); Novel (3); Amusing (7); Pleasing (4); Discordant (8).

The third combination listed is novel, because seldom is it possible to link two pure reds of this type, but the addition of jade green makes the combination possible by holding the two reds together. This amusing combination is suitable for children's rooms, since the two bright colors are associ-

quantity, since a quarter-pound of this glue in solid form, dissolved in a quart of hot water, provides enough sizing to cover 300 square feet of wallpaper. The sizing is applied with a clean bristle brush and must be distributed evenly or you will create a discoloring bulge effect.

Finally, two coats of clear floor varnish are applied, to give a protective coating.

Allow the sizing to dry overnight before applying the first coat of varnish, and a similar time interval before the second protective coat is applied.

## COLOR FOR WALLS

In applying colors to walls, it is important to remember color combinations can create a mood. Many of these moods are related, broadly speaking, to various ages as well as personalities.

Here is a table of color combinations and moods. They are not matched in order; for your own amusement and interest, match them yourself, checking against the correct answers furnished.

**TULIP AND DAISIES**
Another adaptation of a Pennsylvania Dutch design that would look well on a wall.

ated with circuses and toys.

Colors favored in warmer climates are more brilliant than those popular in colder climates. In southern California and Florida there is far more freedom in the use of bright colors than elsewhere.

## Painting on Walls

When you set about painting on the walls of a room, you must first prepare the wall. If you are repainting a wall that already has been painted, clean the surface with any good paint cleaner, available at your paint supply store. If the wall has not previously been painted, apply a coat of primer to seal it; if the wall has been painted before, it does not need resealing with a primer coat unless there are bare patches where paint has chipped or peeled off.

You will need spackling compound to fill in cracks, holes, etc., in the wall before using a priming coat. These openings should be spackled and then shellacked before priming.

For cracks of major size, use a patching compound of plaster and white cement, first knocking loose the crumbling plaster around the edge of the crack. In clearing the loose plaster, make the gap wider in the interior of the wall than at the outer surface. In this way your patch will be held in place more securely.

Use semi-gloss or flat paint for the extensive wall surface, and add any decorative designs you may plan to use in enamel finish. A sealing primer, and enamel, semi-gloss or flat finishes are

STENCILS DID IT

The flowers on this wall have been applied by stenciling. This easy method permits you to create your own original wall designs. For this purpose we recommend the flower patterns in Chapter 2. In a child's room, animals, clowns, and other gay figures would give the right touch.

readily available at paint supply stores.

To protect yourself from dripping paint as you work, slit the center of a 6-inch piece of cardboard, such as the backing which comes in shirts that have

233

been laundered. Run the handle of the paintbrush through the slit, so that the cardboard acts as a shield between the paintbrush bristles and the handle, preventing the paint from running down your arm. In painting a wall, of course, start at the top and paint down!

Enamel paints, such as you would use in the decorative motifs, are generally thick enough so that they spread evenly without dripping. If you find your enamel finish too thick for ready application, thin it with mineral spirits rather than with turpentine, which removes the gloss from the enamel.

If you find you have made the enamel too thin, allow it to stand uncovered; the turpentine will separate from the mixture and evaporate. Use when the proper consistency has developed.

### How to Apply Stencils

In applying cutout stencil figures to walls—or to furniture, for that matter—apply your cutouts with masking tape or Scotch tape to the surface you are decorating. Use a quick-drying enamel. Have a stenciling brush for each color you use; they're obtainable at paint stores. (If you wish to avoid this expense, make up a little ball the size of a half-dollar, using a lint-free muslin cover over a core of cotton; dip just the bottom of the ball into the paint and apply it by patting it hard against the surface you are coloring, always working from the top down; make up a ball for each color).

In using enamel finishes to paint stencils on walls or furniture, pour off

the oil which you find at the top of the can and use only the thick pigment (save the oil for future use in a clean container and pour it back into the can when you've finished your stencil work). Wipe your stencil brush or cotton ball almost clean of paint before you apply it to the cutout area left open by your stencil; paint from an overloaded brush will have the same tendency to run as paint from a mixture that is too liquid.

### Wallpaper and New Materials

Colors and designs on wallpaper should, of course, suit the personality of the occupants of the room. A playroom, which is apt to be a masculine rendezvous, is attractive in natural finish woods. Wallpapers which come close to the appearance of natural wood finishes can be used also.

Among the new materials is a plastic which offers a three-dimensional texture—yet it has the consistency of linoleum, comes in rolls of wallpaper width, is hung like wallpaper, and may be painted like wood. Another is a wood veneer, applied to fabric backing, which looks like wood paneling on your wall. Tile surfaces of cork and leather are also available; these are practical but fairly expensive.

### FOR THE CHILDREN'S ROOM

In providing colors for the walls and floors of children's rooms, consider the age and sex of the children. Girls are apt to prefer colors different from those that boys like.

In the children's room, give voice to the child's color preferences—not your own. Research among children shows that girls prefer blue and red, in that order, above other colors—boys prefer red and then blue. Yellow is favored somewhat in a child's early years, but loses its appeal as a child grows older; green on the other hand tends to increase in popularity, with added years. Younger children show a more spontaneous reaction to intense colors than do older children; grayed colors are unappealing to them. Warm colors are favored over such cold colors as blue-green and violet.

So far as color combinations are concerned, children prefer the combination of yellow and violet to any other; then orange and blue, and yellow and blue. Red and green are preferred to red and blue-green. It will be noted that true complementary color combinations are less favored by children than near-complements.

Favorite three-color combinations among children include: red, orange and yellow; green, blue and violet; blue, red and violet; orange, green and violet; red, yellow and blue; orange, blue and red; blue, green and red.

A good color combination for girls in that growing-up stage just before the so-called "sub-deb" age would be a pale gold and turquoise, with accents of rose and blue.

## Selecting Designs

In selecting designs, too, let the chil-

dren express their own taste. For example, a very clever pattern was created by a young boy who was asked to use his imagination to draw ideas from anything he had seen. The youngster came up with one sketch in pale pink with accent notes of red spots, and another with a dark pink background with white spots showing through. It turned out that these sketches represented his respective recollections of—measles and chicken-pox!

Not all the ideas of a child are so apt —but they represent the individuality

**THE UNICORN**

A little girl who is fond of fairy tales will appreciate this unicorn design in her room. One of the most colorful animals in world folklore, the unicorn has two symbolic meanings: he is the defender of maidens against all enemies of virtue, and he is credited with miraculous healing powers.

which should be given opportunity and scope.

I know one mother who let a youngster participate in decorating the nursery. She painted the lower half of the wall in a different color from the upper half and decorated it with a random scatter pattern of her three-year-old's hand prints in various colors, including

black; the inevitable addition of wall smudges harmonizes nicely!

For a little girl's nursery, it is a good idea to hang the mirror which comes with a dresser set at a low level so the young miss can ogle herself to her feminine heart's content. But here, too, decoration can be used—right on the mirror glass—to conceal the fingermarks which otherwise may keep mother eternally busy!

A mythological unicorn might well serve as a design motif. So too can a peacock which may be drawn by following the steps indicated in the illustration, using compass, ruler and French curve. The peacock, of course, gives you full rein in the use of color.

The child's nursery offers wonderful possibilities in trying your hand at painting murals. You can paint right on the plaster, using the lower half of the wall and maintaining the upper half in solid color as a unifying element. If you're timorous about such a project, a slab of masonite may be decorated and

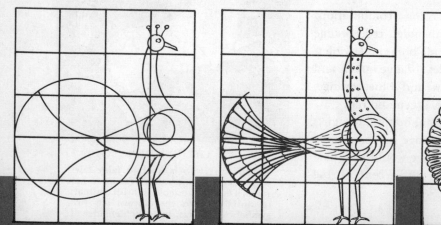
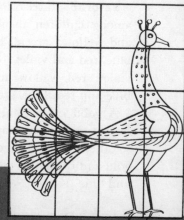

### DRAWING A PEACOCK IN THREE STEPS

One circle guides you in constructing the tail, another sets the outline for the body. All you need is a ruler, compass, and a French curve to draw this peacock. Or you can trace the figure of the finished bird. See Chapter 2 for another peacock on simpler lines, as well as animals and other birds.

attached to the wall, in an area, say, between two windows. This has the advantage of being removable. If you paint on the plaster, use oil paint; cheaper grades are apt to fade after a year's time.

In the little girl's nursery, an Indian princess may be your theme; or the toucan bird, kid or rabbit. To increase your design figure from the size of a small sketch to the larger area involved in decorating a wall, follow the procedure of "squaring off" described in Chapter 2. Divide the small design sketch into numbered squares, and then apply the same number of squares to the larger area to be decorated; copy the parts of the figure that appear in each square into the corresponding square on the larger surface.

Probably no room in the house gives you as much freedom and fun in selecting and applying decorative designs as the child's room. For the child who

loves merry-go-rounds, a sketch of a carousel can be combined with figures of the typical merry-go-round creatures scattered across the wall. These can even be cut out of colored paper, and appliquéd to the wall if you prefer.

Another idea for the nursery is to sketch your own home in different colors. For example, the house pictures shown can be repeated in four color

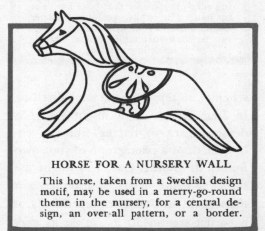

**HORSE FOR A NURSERY WALL**

This horse, taken from a Swedish design motif, may be used in a merry-go-round theme in the nursery, for a central design, an over-all pattern, or a border.

HOME IN COLORS

These pictures show how shading and solid black areas can convey different impressions of the house and garden. Color treatment can do even more to give you variety in the use of the same basic figure. This house and garden—or a picture of your own dwelling—can be painted in playroom or child's room as it appears in spring, summer, fall, and winter by changing the color scheme in each instance.

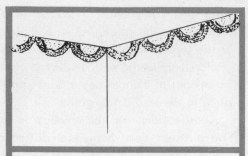

**A DOILY CANOPY**

You can create this canopy-like effect along the upper wall of a room by applying cake-plate doilies that have been cut in half. The white, perforated-border doilies, matching the white of the ceiling, can be used successfully where there is no ceiling molding.

schemes, to represent the same dwelling in four seasons. You might get your design figure by tracing from an enlargement of a photograph of your own home. In another case, you might use the same figure—a dog, or a soldier, or a nursery-rhyme character—repetitively, as a border treatment; if you do so, vary the figure by changing the color slightly —add a little more white as you fill in each figure. In this way you get variety without too much confusion of color contrast.

In planning a design for a repeating wall pattern, remember that too small a figure will look "lost" on a large wall area, while too large a design unit will seem clumsy. In a baby's room, gauge the size of your figures by the size of an infant's field of vision. Don't create your border design by diligently tracing one well-designed figure fifty times in a row—learn to create and use your own symbols in decoration.

## Border of Doilies

One unusual idea in borders, applied to a girl's bedroom, is the use of proper cake-plate doilies, cut in half, as a border for the upper wall where it meets the ceiling. These white, perforated-border doilies match the ceiling in color, and create an effect somewhat like a canopy.

Painting borders on such an area would be a difficult problem physically. From the standpoint of the child's interest, the decoration of the nursery floor can be a more appealing matter to tackle. For the child young enough to play with non-mechanical trains, it might be amusing to him to have make-believe tracks painted right on the floor, together with stations and the landscape that go with it. Large squares in a two-color checkerboard pattern, appropriate to the color scheme of the room, will help the child find use for his large wooden blocks as oversize checkers.

## A Picture Window

A stained-glass effect can lend a novel touch to a child's room, when applied to one pane of a window. Pieces of colored cellophane—available from most theatrical supply stores—can be used to create the design.

Cut strips of cardboard, using two strips stapled together to serve as a frame to hold the colored cellophane in place. By cutting the cardboard and the cellophane strips into shapes which piece together into simple designs, you can achieve a picture that will resemble

238

the more complicated arrangement shown in the illustration of a stained glass window. The cardboard strips are then colored and glued to the glass window pane, with attractive color effects created as the light comes through the cellophane.

## THE PLAYROOM

Next to the children's room, the playroom lends itself most readily to imaginative decoration. A man I know with nautical taste has a playroom fitted up as a "Ship Room" — and occasionally makes it serve as a dining room. Stairs down to the playroom are made into a gangplank, with rubber matting; one wall is decorated as a seascape, with clouds in the sky on the upper half and waves on the lower half; ship's flags are wafted from the walls, and a canvas draped across the cellar ceiling creates a reminder of the after-deck of a vessel. Stanchions and spars lend realism to the atmosphere. Toy anchors serve as centerpiece on the table and hold candles. He calls it the "S.S. *Dunroven*."

For a seagoing atmosphere in your own playroom, the basic elements of an ocean liner are compressed into the simple ship motif illustrated. This motif

**SIMPLE SHIP DESIGN**

A few basic parts of an ocean liner—funnels and passenger cabin windows—tell enough of a story in themselves to serve as a decorative design in a rumpus room carrying out a ship theme.

**CELLOPHANE IMITATES STAINED GLASS**

The heavy black lines shown can be made of cardboard strips that, stapled together, serve as a frame to hold the colored cellophane in place, thus forming a picture window.

239

Design From Early American Pressed Glass, Midwestern

L. ROSS

**STEAMCOACH AND STEAMBOAT DESIGNS.** These designs of early steam mode
You can use them with or withou

Design From Early American Pressed Glass...Midwestern

L. ROSS

will add a quaint touch to a playroom.
he decorative borders.

**FOR THE PLAYROOM BAR**

For the playroom bar, how about an elephant design—painted in no other color but pink. A cutout, appliquéd to bar or wall, is one convenient way of handling this theme. The elephant at the left, who looks somewhat the worse for wear, might be located high on the wall or on the door, in a position to survey the entire scene. An elephant is also a happy choice for a nursery.

suggests a point that is basic in achieving good but simple design treatment: Invent motifs which contain the essence of the form, rather than a detailed replica. For example, the tulips of the Pennsylvania Dutch, in a few basic familiar outlines, are easily recognized, although the texture is not detailed, nor is the exact relationship of petals made clear.

This point is also illustrated in the skiing figure shown. This will be appropriate for the playroom of a family fond of winter sports.

For the playroom which includes a bar, pink elephants (perhaps as cutouts of cork applied to a masonite bar) become original if one of their number finds his way somewhat bleary-eyed onto the wall behind the bar, where he can mournfully survey his fellows—and the assembled company.

Why not decorate the walls of a man's

den with card motifs? (You can choose between painting them on, and mounting them with decoupage.) Be free with your use of colors for the playing-card figures of king, queen or jack, and stylize the figure to suit your taste and skill. The theme is good for a playroom or for a living room in a home much devoted to card-playing.

Letting your hobbies govern your decoration is a sure way of making your home pleasant to the members of the family and will express your personality to visitors.

If golf is the key to a man's happiness —give him golf, in the form of a golf-club or golf-ball motif! If it's fishing, his dry-fly discards can be put to decorative use; often they are very colorful. These could be attached to a fishnet wall hanging, with other reminders of happy times angling. Or why not have a picture of Papa fishing from the lower wall and catching a "whopper" on the baseboard?

An aviation enthusiast may be cheered with silhouettes of planes in different colors, painted directly on, or appliquéd to, the walls. The sailing enthusiast can have a playroom in which waves ripple over the lower walls. The duck-hunter will enjoy duck decoys on the baseboard of the wall—or on the lower wall itself: If you can acquire a decoy or two for home decoration, so much the better!

And the gardener will be enchanted with flowers apparently growing out of the wallboard onto lower-wall areas.

For the lover of Paris and sidewalk cafés—and the two wars have given us many men who hold a soft spot for that light-hearted city!—iron furniture reminiscent of outdoor dining can be painted on a playroom bar, and a gaily striped awning can cheer the upper wall. Or the bar or liquor cabinet can be painted with bottle labels, or actual labels can be mounted in an interesting decoupage from your supply.

For the floor of a cellar playroom, a shuffleboard is an enlivening feature which will provide sport indoors. The cellar playroom is also made more livable by painting in windows—sometimes we miss this familiar feature of a room more than we realize in setting up a living space "downstairs."

## THE BATHROOM

Another room that lends itself to decoration is the bathroom. Once upon a time it was always sanitary white.

### PLAYING CARD DECORATION

Jack of Hearts makes a colorful wall panel decoration for cardroom, den, playroom, or nursery. The drawing is easy to copy. The color scheme might have gold or silver as a background. Cap can be red and green, hair brown, face and hands and axe handle white, tunic gold and two tones of blue, one sleeve and one stocking dark blue, other sleeve, heart, sash and sword red, shoes black. Other details can be filled in from the colors already suggested.

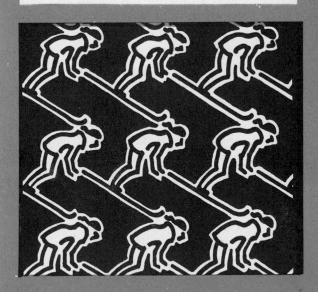

### PATTERN FOR SKIERS

If you enjoy skiing, you might decorate the playroom—its doors, panels on the walls, or other parts—with this over-all design or a figure taken from it.

**WINDOWS IN BASEMENT PLAYROOM**

If you don't have windows in your downstairs playroom, you can easily paint them
on your walls, looking out on a vista that fits your fancy. Sections of decorated tiles
are also excellent for this effect.

Now it is changed. Colored tile and hand-painted pictures or decals of fish and sea life have lifted the face of this sanctum; and wallpaper and linoleum have also come into common use. Some appealing figures for bathroom walls are shown in the accompanying illustrations.

But for a personal touch, why not a few umbrellas at various angles, with the cloth parts of the umbrella made of bits of real fabric in different patterns which are pasted on and varnished over? Over the umbrella silvery streaks of rain pour down (radiator paint will do it).

In one home I have visited, the host had painted his name in red, white and black on a plastic shower curtain. In another, the master of the house has set up a pattern of blue raindrops on a grayish plastic material for his shower curtain.

For just one touch of color, the use of a simple band of color around the plastered upper wall, where the lower half is tiled, will produce a bright note of interest.

## THE KITCHEN

The kitchen offers opportunities for color, too. An appropriate motto about food can be inscribed on a wall area—one such, taken from the Pennsylvania Dutch, is included in Chapter 4 among the ideas for lettered mottoes.

Go further; write a favorite, simple recipe on the wall if the area permits. Embellish it with a colored illustration of the dish painted by hand or cut from one of the better magazines and pasted on the wall and covered over with clear spar varnish for durability. Or let caricatured kitchen utensils or food march across your walls. Other suggestions that may be worked out with decals will be given a little later.

## OTHER ROOMS

Living rooms and bedrooms present more of a challenge, for there your wall must be suited to your furniture. If your room is built around antiques, then you may want to use decorations on your walls that suit the spirit of the furniture. In a room with Indian rugs, motifs of Indian origin will be appropriate. If the room is an informal one, several of the designs we have suggested for the playroom may be in order, or some of the folk decorations pictured in earlier chapters might be used. But most people will probably prefer a more dignified tone in living room and bedroom, and so we shall recommend some paint and wallpaper treatments without designs.

In your bedroom, you can paint the

SEA SCENES FOR A BATHROOM

Pictures of marine life and sailing vessels lend a light and airy touch that seems appropriate for bathrooms. These same scenes will serve for decorating a child's room or a playroom.

wall against which the bed stands in a color to match the wood of the bed—this is particularly appropriate with modern furniture—rather than the same as the other three walls. If you have a painted wood bedroom suite—or if you are painting an old set of furniture—give it a ground coat to match the color on one wall and paint the other three walls in a harmonious color.

A bedroom or breakfast nook with wallpaper of bold-sized ivy leaf pattern can use a green the color of the leaves on the opposite wall—or on three walls.

On bedroom walls, a color motif taken from the rugs has a unifying effect. It is particularly effective to do so when the rugs are of Indian designs, with the distinguishing bright Indian

*(Top)*     MAKE YOUR FIREPLACE GAY

Don't forget the fireplace in decorating your living room. Tiles decorated to your taste, as explained in Chapter 7, will enhance the charm of the room greatly. The designs might be tied in with those you paint on furnishings.

*(Bottom)*     SOMETHING DIFFERENT IN CORNICES

Many small features of a room with excellent possibilities for decoration are often overlooked. Cornices, for example, will be much more attractive when you treat them with color and designs.

ENLIVENING KITCHEN CABINETS

You can repeat the same design, as illustrated, have variety of designs, or use the whole kitchen to portr parts of a scene, such as a countryside with people a buildings and trees.

colors which can give life to a wall area.

On the other hand, the wall decorations can serve as color inspiration for other furnishings of the bedroom.

The decoupage described in the chap-

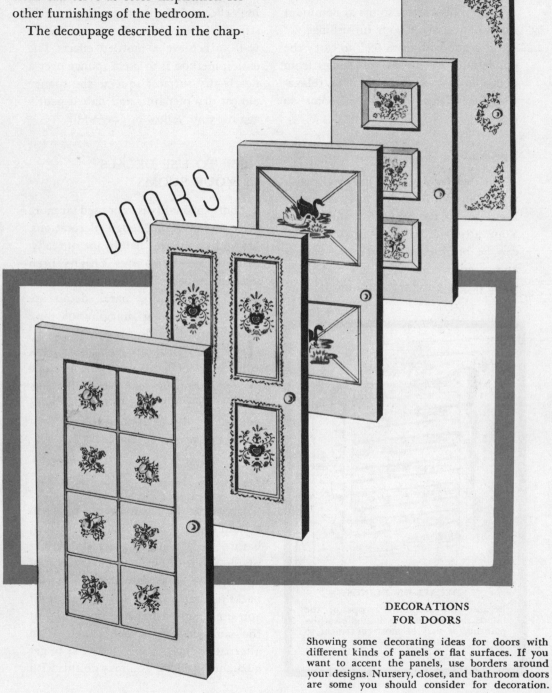

DOORS

## DECORATIONS FOR DOORS

Showing some decorating ideas for doors with different kinds of panels or flat surfaces. If you want to accent the panels, use borders around your designs. Nursery, closet, and bathroom doors are some you should consider for decoration.

ter on furniture decoration may aptly be applied to wall treatments, for example. From these illustrations, in turn, you may select colors as dominant notes or accents in your furnishings.

It's a good idea, we feel, to carry the colors and the decorative themes from bedroom to bathroom; there's a relaxation in living with these rooms so closely unified.

## The Attic

For the study or attic, gray walls with red or brown accents are a tasty combination. So, too, are yellow and brown. Your attic, if dark as most attics are, can be brightened by painting ceiling and window wall in yellow and other walls in gray; the wall around the win-

**DECALS ON BLINDS**
Because the horizontal strips of the blinds are hard to keep motionless while painting, it may be most convenient to use decals here.

dow is usually the darkest, as the light streams in to brighten the other walls, and the brighter yellow has an equalizing effect. For an appealing touch, stipple the brown accent over a yellow wall to achieve a mottled effect. The easiest method is to use a sponge over a nearly dry surface; squeeze the sponge almost dry of paint, and dab it gently against your yellow or gray wall.

## HOW TO USE DECALS IN YOUR ROOMS

Your personality is expressed far more fully by original design decorations, drawn by yourself, than by use of ready-made decorative features. This has been stressed repeatedly throughout this book. On the other hand, decals are showing increasing imagination and variety, and they do provide a speedy, neat and uniform ornamentation. Also, your choice of decals still provides scope for expression of your taste. The suggestions that follow for decoration with decals may also be applied to the use of designs of your own, naturally.

### Designs on Doors

Doors can be treated with decals in certain rooms of the home—the nursery, bathrooms, closets, or playroom. Other places where they may add a note of appropriate color are on chests, walls, backs of chairs, in the bathroom, etc. If you use them on paneled doors, repeat the same design in each panel, or in alternate panels in such a way as to get a balancing effect. You may do this with

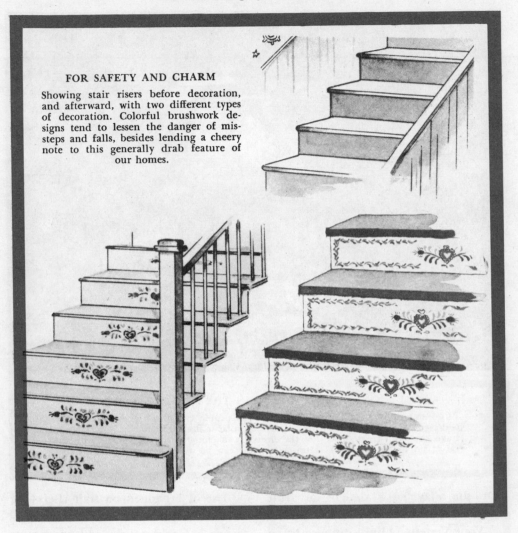

**FOR SAFETY AND CHARM**

Showing stair risers before decoration, and afterward, with two different types of decoration. Colorful brushwork designs tend to lessen the danger of missteps and falls, besides lending a cheery note to this generally drab feature of our homes.

or without borders for each panel. For an unpaneled door, a border decal may be used to set off the corners, or may be bent around the knob as an outline.

The kitchen offers wide scope for use of decals. Most kitchens are distinguished by lack of blank wall space, as more and more homemakers adopt both overhead cabinets and cabinet bases to compress storage and work-space into the small kitchen of modern home or apartment. Too often, these cabinets are treated in a glossy white—easy to clean, but uninspiring to the woman who spends a great deal of her time there.

One way to give the kitchen a change of pace in color is through the use of colorful decals suggestive of any part of the world fancied by the woman of the house — Mexican, Pennsylvania Dutch, French, Scandinavian or some other.

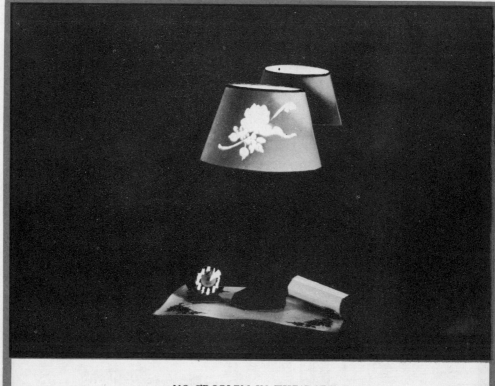

**NO PROBLEM IN THE DARK**

Luminous paint is helpful on stairs, but few people ever think of using it to paint a design on their lamps. In the picture, the plastic flashlight and bedside table mat have also been treated, so that the sleeper awakening during the night will surely be at no loss in the dark. Luminous paint can be used in many different colors.

Or she may favor designs or fruit, flowers, etc.

Your Venetian blinds can also be enlivened by use of decals, on alternate strips. To dramatize your window further (and to avoid the use of dirt-catching drapes), build a frame or "shadow-box" of thin playwood with scalloped edges—if you lack the tools, a lumber dealer who sells the wood will cut the scalloped piece for you at a modest cost. With this combination of blinds and frame, you can work out attractively related decorative motifs.

Use of ornament on stair risers—the surface between steps on a stairway—lends a bright touch, and encourages you to use lighter-colored backgrounds than you might normally apply on the steps, particularly for attic or cellar stairs. This introduces a valuable safety factor, as well as an ornamental touch. With a decal on each riser, you can be assured of uniformity in your decorative motifs which might be difficult to obtain because of the cramped position required to paint the stair risers.

A practical alternative idea in decorating stairs, which does allow you to take advantage of the space offered by stairways to express yourself with your own decorative designs, is the use of "luminous paint"—the phosphorescent paint which "glows" in the dark. The advantage of this new type of paint, from the standpoint of accident prevention, is obvious. It is recommended for use on stairways or elsewhere—however, only in locations which are subject to strong daylight or artificial light for a good period of time each day. Exposed to strong light for five to ten minutes, the paint will store up light energy like a storage battery, and obtains its "glowing" power in this fashion.

## A LAST WORD:
## COLOR IN YOUR LIFE

In the preceding pages I have touched upon many of the ways you can use color in the home and make your surroundings more a part of you as you do so.

My main interest has been devoted to colors, and to materials on which colors can be realized. At the same time, I have attempted to avoid the province of the interior decorator.

Beyond the walls of your home, there are also other places where color can be brought into your life, both in the figurative and the literal sense. In the schoolroom, correct use of color protects your child's precious vision and gives a proper atmosphere for study; in office buildings and factories, it can provide a stimulating, morale-building background for more effective work. It has an important role to play in hospitals, churches, and elsewhere.

Indeed, there are few limits to the use of color in our lives. The airplane, for example, was a drab passenger conveyance when I was given the first opportunity to apply color appeal in an interior, back in 1935. Today, railroads and ocean vessels and buses follow the lead of the airlines in using color effectively, and there are new uses of color —a new understanding of color—everywhere we turn.

Living-room heaters now blossom forth in textured, cheery colors suited to modern furniture woods and fabrics; vacuum cleaners, refrigerators, radios and a host of other things for the home now provide effective and attractive color. Even phonograph records are colored to the mood and style of the music, and typewriters and other objects long content with a single dingy color seek favor in our eyes.

If homemaker and businessman alike, after reading this book, can project, not only to their homes, but to other aspects of their surroundings as well, the appreciation of color as a means of enriching our lives, I shall feel satisfied that I have awakened a train of thought of broadest significance.